What People Are Saying About
No More Christian Nice Guy

"John Eldredge gave men permission to be 'wild at heart.' Paul Coughlin shows us how to do it. This book is a road map to a larger life."

—**David Murrow**, Author of *Why Men Hate Going to Church*

"When Jesus walked into the temple and saw the moneychangers, he didn't say, 'Hey, fellas, have a nice day!' He threw them out on their rears. I applaud Paul's important work to help us realize what a real man is all about. Real men will read Paul Coughlin's book."

—**Dr. Kevin Leman**, Bestselling author of *The Birth Order Book* and *Women Who Try Too Hard*

"Paul Coughlin is challenging our thinking on what it means to be God's man in the twenty-first century. The apostle Paul pens in 1 Corinthians 16:13, 'Act like men.' That begs the question, What is a man? Coughlin is asking that question. This book is his excellent answer."

—**Emerson Eggerichs, Ph.D.**, Author of *Love and Respect: The Love She Most Desires, the Respect He Desperately Needs*

"Paul has some bold, powerful, and even shocking words for the church. If the church wants to get a handle on rampant divorce and infidelity, Paul has some words of wisdom we dare not ignore."

—**Dave Meurer**, Author of *Good Spousekeeping: A His and Hers Guide to Couplehood*

"*No More Christian Nice Guy* is a must-read for every Christian man; yes! A provocative approach to exposing t⬚⬚⬚⬚⬚⬚ ⬚⬚⬚⬚⬚⬚ ⬚⬚⬚⬚ ⬚⬚me point or another, adopted in our att⬚⬚⬚⬚ ⬚⬚⬚⬚⬚⬚⬚ ⬚⬚⬚⬚d powerful challenge to true biblical m⬚⬚⬚⬚⬚⬚ ⬚⬚⬚⬚⬚ ⬚⬚r godly men with a personality."

—**Marcos Perez**, Associate Publish⬚⬚⬚, ⬚⬚⬚ ⬚⬚⬚⬚⬚

Books by Paul Coughlin

No More Christian Nice Guy

Married . . . But Not Engaged

STUDY GUIDE

NO MORE

YOUR PERSONAL BATTLE PLAN

CHRISTIAN

FOR THE GOOD GUY REBELLION

NICE GUY

PAUL COUGHLIN

BETHANYHOUSE

MINNEAPOLIS, MINNESOTA

No More Christian Nice Guy Study Guide
Copyright © 2006
Paul Coughlin

Cover design by Lookout Design, Inc.

Published by Bethany House Publishers
11400 Hampshire Avenue South
Bloomington, Minnesota 55438

Bethany House Publishers is a division of
Baker Publishing Group, Grand Rapids, Michigan.

Printed in the United States of America

ISBN-13:   978-0-7642-0222-3
ISBN-10:   0-7642-0222-7

Library of Congress Cataloging-in-Publication Data

Coughlin, Paul T.
   No more Christian nice guy. Study guide : your personal battle plan for the good guy rebellion / Paul Coughlin.
      p.   cm.
   Summary: "A twelve-lesson study manual to help good—not nice—Christian guys become less passive and more assertive. Features study questions for individual use and suggestions for small-group leaders"—Provided by publisher.
   Includes bibliographical references.
   ISBN 0-7642-0222-7 (pbk.)
   1. Coughlin, Paul T. No more Christian nice guy.   2. Christian men—Religious life.
3. Men (Christian theology)—Biblical teaching.   I. Title.
   BV4528.2.C6733   2006
   248.8'42—dc22

                                                              2006013581

ACKNOWLEDGMENTS

This Study Guide wouldn't be as helpful if it weren't for the aid of the *No More Christian Nice Guy Study Guide* Focus Group, a brave group of men and women who shared their pain, hope, and faith. A special thanks to Tom Suttle, Barbara Wiedenbeck (I can still taste the lamb), and Bob Hurless.

And thank you to all the Christian Nice Guys struggling to become Christian Good Guys. Your stories may be commonplace to you, but they have stirred a fire in others. You have filled the ranks of the Good Guy Rebellion for generations to come.

PAUL COUGHLIN hosts a radio talk show in southern Oregon on The Dove (*www.thedove.us*) and is the author of *Secrets, Plots, and Hidden Agendas: What You Don't Know About Conspiracy Theories.* Paul has been interviewed by C-SPAN, the *New York Times,* and numerous radio and television stations across the country. His articles have appeared in many publications, including *New Man, Faithworks,* and *Ministries Today.* He has also been editor of a weekly newspaper and a radio station program director. A former Christian Nice Guy, Paul is a Life Coach, especially for passive men. He is happily married and the father of two boys and one girl. The Coughlin family lives in Oregon. See Paul's Web site at *www.Christianniceguy.com*

TABLE OF CONTENTS

Are churches really inundated with aggressive, obnoxious, self-centered man-jerks who need to change their barbaric ways? This is what you would conclude if you went to an average church service. You would likely hear men being told to be more gentle, combat their selfish ways, confront their nasty competitiveness, become less willful and opinionated, and control their dangerous emotions and related passions.

Sure, there are men in church who are too rough, angry, nasty. But they are a minority, practically an endangered species. If you see one in church, stand next to him and have someone snap a picture. Put it in your scrapbook. Get his autograph. Both might be worth good money someday.

On average, Christianity and related men's ministry are preaching to a marginal group of guys on Sunday mornings. Our pews host men with different inclinations and hang-ups. They aren't willful, opinionated, or passionate enough. They are men who have been rendered drab by a religious tendency to erase their individuality and a discernible pulse. They're flat-lined, robotic, low-voltage men whose shut-down personalities are a far cry from the founders of our faith.

It's not just Christianity either. Rabbi Shmuley Boteach complains about the same maddening tendency within Judaism. "As many of my friends have become more religious, they have allowed their personalities to atrophy . . . Their sex lives have been undermined by inhibition and a discomfort with carnal indulgence, to the conformist trends of the religious clergy which has made so many rabbis . . . dull and uninspiring. Religion has snuffed out the spark of many of its adherents."

Church is host to generations of nice, pleasant, and pliable men, careful not to ruffle feathers—especially *female* feathers. They're rule-bound. Disciples of status quo. They have been trained well by our culture, especially our churches, to bring harm to no one or no thing. They worship at the altar of other people's approval. This is their life—and it sure isn't living.

They have a light approach toward life, which unfortunately for the weak and the timid includes blatant injustice. They are nice and amiable in the face of evil, making them victims and reducing those who are charged with their care to victim status as well. They may well be considered accomplices.

On one hand they make great neighbors because they live by all the man-made rules we heap on each other. Their etiquette is astounding. Their lawns are green and manicured, and if they have a dog, it likely won't go number two on your lawn. In America, this means a lot.

But if you're looking for someone who can help you through a Dark Night of the Soul, he's not your man.

As popular writer Philip Yancey observed, "Evangelicals can be the kind of responsible citizens most people appreciate as neighbors but don't want to spend much time with."

Part of this is due to the fact that many evangelical men don't possess much energy or vitality. They think it's Christian to embrace low-voltage living, to become sideline people. Their wives are often more interesting and alive than they are. Many complain how passive these men are, which is peculiar since many churches unintentionally guide them toward passivity. Our churches are anvil factories, not hammer factories. No wonder a great man like Abraham Lincoln attended church but was careful never to become a member.

Happiness eludes such men, but they can't admit it. It's not "Christian." They don't think it's okay to be real and human. Many are *ashamed* to be human, to be made in God's image. They don't know how to be authentic.

What makes this problem so ironic, dangerous, damaging, and, yep, sinful, is that these men hardly behave like the real Jesus, the person they claim to follow. I'm not talking about hypocrisy either, the ailment that plagues us all. Hypocrisy is when we claim to adhere to the right ideal but don't in real life. No, we aren't even aiming at the right ideal, the real man himself. Right now our ideal is to be the nicest people on earth. Our goal should be to become the best *good* people on earth. The gap between nice and good is as far as the east is from the west. The difference between our fictitious Nice Nazarene who we currently follow and the real Jesus we largely ignore is dangerously wide as well.

So why do churches tell the mass of nice, compliant, and submissive men to be more patient and kind to a fault, when they really need to hear a completely different message? That's where *No More Christian Nice Guy* comes in.

It went to the heart of this problem, apparently very deeply. Wrote one reader:

"*No More Christian Nice Guy* is the most applicable and real take on Christian masculinity to date. It surfaced many of the lies the church and my parents (often unintentionally) embedded in me at a young age, forcing me to wrestle with my own version of the 'Christian Nice Guy' syndrome. Coughlin's transparent heart seeks to aid hurting men, while his personal recovery story is filled with life-giving honesty."

Readers also noticed that it was different than other books on this topic. Wrote one struggling Christian Nice Guy, "I know that evangelicals write a lot of books on living the victorious life. Your book seems different. More real. . . . I wonder if sometimes I have twisted theology to avoid really living life."

Other readers tell me how *No More Christian Nice Guy* takes the life of Christian men and lifts it to a whole new level, above what they've experienced before at church or during men's functions. They wanted a Study Guide to help them sink this message deeper into their souls.

WHO IS THIS FOR?

This Study Guide is not an attempt to give you yet another Christian obligation. If that's how you feel, then put this Study Guide down now. Run! This isn't dreaded homework. And if you're the kind of guy who needs to be told what to think, then this Study Guide definitely isn't for you. There's no crooked religious finger pointing at you, trying to shame you and turn you into a nice little boy.

This Study Guide is designed to meet the needs of individuals, small groups, and even larger groups like Sunday school classes. I hope prisoners get together and ingest it too. You'd be amazed at just how many passive men snap (i.e., passive-aggressive behavior) and commit heinous acts that they regret for the rest of their lives.

It's remarkable (and maddening) how quickly we forget what we need to remember to really live. This Study Guide will reinforce the truths you've already been exposed to and want to stick in your marrow. Some may want to use it as a devotional.

This Study Guide is for you, Nice Guys in general and Nice Guys with a Christian excuse in particular. It's also for the women who know them, love them, and sometimes want to scream at them. It's for the kids who are abandoned by their checked-out father, a guy who smiles a lot but shows through various ways that it's not a smile born from happiness, joy, peace, or contentment. Babies smile when they have gas pains. Nice Guys smile from pain as well. Their kids sense this. I'm here to tell you that your senses are right. This Study Guide will help hone your senses and inoculate you from becoming a Nice Guy (or Nice Girl) in the future.

It's also for guys who are already Christian Good Guys. They will have their character affirmed and strengthened. And they'll be better able to help their brothers who struggle with niceness, this vice that masquerades as a virtue.

This Study Guide is designed to help you become the right kind of dangerous, like the Jesus that is found in history, who is different from the one many of us have found in Sunday school. Otherwise you're no match for evil and its ploys, for manipulators of many stripes and flavors. This is one reason Jesus told us to be wise as serpents. The same word for *wise* has been translated as *shrewd* and *cunning*. Yet we associate these character traits with criminals, which is one of the biggest mistakes many Christians make. Get ready to become the right kind of cunning, the good kind of shrewd. Your life will take off.

WHAT YOU'LL NEED

You'll need a copy of *No More Christian Nice Guy*, otherwise this Study Guide just won't make sense. You'll also want a notebook to write down longer explorations into the Christian Nice Guy problem. My favorite notebook by far is Moleskine (pronounced *mol-a-skeen'-a*, don't ask me why). Most major bookstores carry them. And if you read the promotional material they come with, you'll find that keen-eyed Hemingway, who hated pretense—though not as much as Jesus—used one as well. I hope this helps you cut through malarkey. Moleskine are more expensive, but having gone through dozens of other notebooks, I can say they are worth it.

And notebooks have a way of becoming among your most important possessions. Wrote the apostle Paul to young Timothy, "When you come, bring the cloak that I left with Carpus at Troas, and my scrolls, especially the parchments" (2 Timothy 4:13).

Consider using a digital recorder too. I carry one most everywhere. I've found that sometimes the answers to soul-mending questions don't come right away. Sometimes the nuts of your life are hard to crack at first. You think hard, you search your heart and pray deeply, and still the answers refuse to show themselves. But then, usually during recreation or mundane times like driving, an insight shines. It's bright, yet it's a bit unfocused. It doesn't shout, but it's powerful nonetheless. That's God's grace helping you out. Record it. It will be useful later.

WHAT YOU CAN EXPECT

Each of the twelve lessons include a summary and numerous questions to ponder, helping you to progress out of the Christian Nice Guy ghetto and into the ranks of the Good Guy Rebellion.

Along the way are **Good Guy Workouts,** exercises that help you move from passivity to assertiveness. The move is easier than you might think. You could say it's like climbing a ladder. In fact, that image shows up as a reminder to push past your passivity and do something proactive and assertive. Groups may even want to award a symbolic "Ladder of Assertiveness" whenever a Nice Guy . . .

- Recognizes a moment when he is usually passive and often dishonest
- Responds assertively
- Reminds himself that this is how the real Jesus behaved
- Retells his story to someone else who understands his struggle and celebrates his victory.

Some sections have **Bonus Information,** insights into the Christian Nice Guy problem not found in the *Nice Guy* book.

Look for the **Good Guy Rebellion Roll Call,** letters from readers that help shed additional light on this problem.

You'll also see **Jesus the Naughty Nazarene.** It contains examples of Jesus' tougher language and behavior. If your average Christian man behaved this way, we would label him as naughty and a troublemaker. These examples show just how far off the mark we've gone.

A WORD ABOUT SETTING

I wrote part of this Study Guide on the northwest slope of a nearby hill. Haggis, my puckish cairn terrier, accompanied me. I wanted to get as close to the bone of this topic as I could. I wanted to figure out the best way for men (and women) to take the insights from *No More Christian Nice Guy* and make them their own. To lift it up, wrestle with it, or throw it to the ground if they want. Drink it in, hold it above their head like a sports hero, and dance their own funky dance. Or kick it to the curb.

This Study Guide will help *you* to see *you* more clearly. This is *your* life, full of *your* choices and *your* decisions. Take these ideas and make them part of your DNA. Or part of this week's trash. Become an active agent in your own life—moving yourself toward the best outcome you can help muster, stumbling arm and arm with your good God while discarding the dangerous notion that you have to do it so perfectly. That's an illusion—and an excuse—that keeps you stuck. Asking the right questions helps you get to you and God.

I'm telling you the setting of this creation because I'd like for you to do the same. Get outside if you can as an individual or a group. Suck some fresh air through your city nostrils, put some sun on your pale, cubicle face. You don't have to climb a hill, scale a north face, or ford a river either. Just go in your backyard or on the patio or lanai. Take up a seat in a park. If someone's next to you, show them the cover and watch their eyes light up. It's fun, and it may lead to an enlightening conversation. Throw down a blanket or tarp somewhere. Getting outside clears your head like smelling salts under the nose of a boxer. There are fewer voices in your noggin to contend with, so answers reveal themselves more readily.

FIELD TESTED

Please know that this Study Guide isn't coming to you raw and untried. Numerous people who found *No More Christian Nice Guy* indispensable joined our Focus Group. This brave clan of men and women helped bring you a better resource through which you'll grow, and I'm grateful to each one of them.

Wrote one member of the Focus Group:

Dear Paul,

Your Study Guide is outstanding. Great information and even better questions. Your straight-forwardness is exactly what we men need to hear. It needs to be shouted from the biggest megaphone there is. Thanks for caring about men.

—Bob

NOTE TO GROUP LEADERS

This material goes deep into people's lives. Like someone pulled from the tide, sometimes seawater needs to come out before that person can breathe again. You are the lifeguard, and they are your people on your beach, flirting with the tide that makes life exhilarating and dangerous. They simply will not learn much about themselves if they don't get wet. So don't try to control the outcome too much. Pray that lies will be exposed and that souls will become teachable and thirsty for insight. Pray they will seek the truth through any obscurity and know that such a condition is temporary.

Lives don't go wrong overnight. Success as well as failure leaves a trail, a progression to analyze. And contrary to some church lore, lives usually don't get better overnight either. Be willing to live with unraveled edges: statements that may not be accurate now but may become so later. Let change happen. Let freedom reign.

You are handling people's souls, so you must ensure complete confidentiality during your gatherings. It's a sacred act when battered souls come out of their timid hiding places to reveal their sins and the sins committed against them. Telling people outside your group about what happens during your meetings is a breach in trust and respect. Enforce this policy.

There is one exception: If a man in your group is harming a child or woman, move ASAP. Christian Good Guys protect those in need. Always. The guy may thank you later. Or not. That's his problem. The child or woman will certainly be grateful (it may take time), and your Father in Heaven will be proud.

Groups may also want to read each lesson aloud. This makes it more personal and helps the insights go deeper. Try to bring into your group at least one guy who doesn't fit the Christian Nice Guy mold. But don't go and grab his opposite, some gruff grump who has a mile-wide and an inch-deep opinion about everything. Bring a guy into the group whose first desire when he enters a room isn't to make everyone like him. A guy who's comfortable in his own skin and who knows how to do conflict pretty well. A guy who doesn't have to be right and perfect all the time. A male with a backbone.

Why go through this soul work? Because there's a name for people who realize they aren't helpless in the face of problems and turmoil. People who embrace the gifts and common sense God gave them. Men and women who know that some of what they hear in church isn't true, yet their faith is still strong. They still believe, they still attend because their hearts accommodate human frailty. They recognize that life is often not clean and tidy, that ambiguity often reigns. They are people of courage and faith who hold their ground regardless. People of will, not because they're selfish, but because they have normal wants and needs, and they know it's no sin admitting this. They have been called many names throughout history. Today we call them successful. You aren't used to being successful, Christian Nice Guy. You may even fear it. You're used to finishing in the frustrating middle, where the mass of ordinary "dead" men somehow manage to live. But God didn't call you to be ordinary. He wants you to be like his son, the Divine Dissident. He's the bold

Emancipator from sin, lies, and convenient rationalizations. He has the keys to your freedom, if only you'll release him from the Nice Guy strait-jacket, his mild-mannered Sunday best in which we have him bound.

Paul Coughlin

CHRISTIAN NICE GUYS AREN'T SO NICE

The first chapter of *No More Christian Nice Guy* explains how what we label "nice" is often passivity, fear, and shame in disguise. We will be more like Christ when we stop these messages from coming into our lives and when we exhume them from our troubled hearts and minds. What's more, this lifestyle is full of sin: timid lies, cowardice, nuanced manipulations, and soul-crushing control of others.

Chapter 1 also shows how passive and fearful Christian Nice Guys (CNGs) hear what they want to hear when exposed to the dangerous caricature of "gentle Jesus meek and mild." They don't think they can handle the truth about God and his requirements of them, so they hide behind the Nice Guy Bible (NGB). It's an unauthorized translation read by millions. So the place for you to start this lesson, and each one in this Guide, is to read the chapter. Then go deeper by working your way through the lesson.

DEFINITIONS

Passivity is defined as the quality of being passive, which means you tend to submit or obey without arguing or resisting. When applied to the

Christian Nice Guy problem, it helps to add an additional understanding of this frustrating condition. Passivity is better understood as possessing a dangerously low amount of will, which is a state that leaves you (and those who depend upon you) open to many forms of abuse and manipulation. Will, related to your conscience, common sense, and intuition, can be a form of self-defense, much like antibodies. It can also pave the way toward your freedom.

Take the CNG test beginning on page twenty-one of *No More Christian Nice Guy*. But only do so if you're willing to be honest. Some people don't want to be honest at this point because they don't want to feel bad about themselves. So they tweak their answers. Shun this thinking. Push past these feelings if they come your way. In order to move into a better place, you need to know where you are today. So be honest, and realize that these answers are only temporary. They may be how you feel now, but this doesn't mean you'll always feel this way. That's the good thing about life. It comes one day at a time, and no two days are the same.

Honesty is the beginning of your Christian Good Guy transformation. And when answering each question straight up, don't put yourself down afterward. To err is human. God knows this. Jesus witnessed this and he doesn't condemn you for it. Tell yourself when reviewing your answers, "This is interesting," instead of "I'm always messing up," or related derogatory messages. Remember, it's a sin to bear false witness against another person. It's also wrong to bear false witness against yourself.

Resist the urge to get angry with yourself or others when you review your answers. Anger is a valuable emotion, but it must be harnessed and filtered. (Sometimes anger is the result of fear and a feeling of powerlessness. More on that later.) For now, be honest and look at your answers with a somewhat detached view, the way a scientist analyzes data.

Write down the first answer that comes to mind. If or when you answer yes, ask yourself why. Where did you receive this information? Who told you this information was true?

THE NICE GUY BIBLE (NGB)

Look at the underlined portions of your Bible.

What is their flavor and tone? Chances are, they extol gentle virtues. Yet on the same page, or in the same book, you will likely find examples of more rugged virtues as well.

Why aren't they underlined with the same frequency and fervor?

Did someone encourage you to underline only the gentle portions? If so, do you know why?

HEARING WHAT WE WANT TO HEAR

One reason why we don't catch Jesus' tougher side is because Christian Nice Guys see what they want to see. It's not an accident or oversight. We often gloss over, or pretend not to experience, information that makes us uncomfortable and challenges our thinking.

What is it about his tougher side that scares you?

Why do you think we avoid the very help that has the power to make our lives better?

GOOD GUY WORKOUT

Think about the Jesus you envisioned growing up. Most kids have an image of him, whether or not they grew up in a Christian home.

What does he look like?

What does he communicate with his eyes?

Jesus was essentially homeless and traveled by foot. What do such people look like today?

Is your impression of him different? If so, why do you think this inconsistency exists?

○ After reading chapter 1 in *No More Christian Nice Guy*, come up with a list of CNGs you know or have seen in the media. Then make a list of Christian Good Guys (CGGs). Don't think you're being mean by creating such a comparison. We put people in categories all the time. It's not a sin. You're not creating these lists to condemn anyone. You're doing it to gain greater understanding.

○ What do the guys on the CNG list have in common? What do the guys on the CGG list have in common?

○ How do the guys on one list behave? How about the guys on the other list?

○ Do the guys on each list share any physical features (hairstyle, dress)?

○ Who do you want to be like? More importantly, why?

Make a list of Christian Good Guys throughout history—people who are truth-bearers, regardless of opposition (and this list includes women as well). And don't get tripped up regarding style, or how they went about their important work. Some CGGs are loud, some more reserved.

What qualities do they possess?

How did others treat them?

How did they respond to critics and enemies?

How did they refuse to let their detractors define them?

What does this tell you about people who bear the truth?

GOING DEEPER

Do you think the apostle Paul's admonishment to the Ephesians to be gentle applies to everyone in every circumstance?

What would happen if police officers, defense attorneys, and prison guards always followed this admonishment?

How come such men are allowed to be tough when defending themselves and others, but you don't think you can be?

Where did you get this false message?

Who has told you that you shouldn't exert your will? Why?

 ## GOOD GUY WORKOUT

Becoming Wise / Shrewd / Cunning as Serpents

We often hear parents say they did their best and that their motives were pure when raising their children.

Do you know anyone who does his or her best all the time, every time?

Why do we say this as parents when such a level is unattainable?

There was only one person who had pure motives on planet Earth. Right now he's at the right hand of God intervening on our behalf. Yet for some reason we ascribe to our fellow man pure motives.

Why are we compelled to believe that people possess pure motives when good motives can be sufficient?

I'm asking you to consider these issues because they go to the heart of the Christian Nice Guy problem: naïveté. We leave our lives open to a self-perpetuating cycle of hurt when we harbor naïve understandings of life. This cycle leaves us broken and untrusting. Our souls get seared, we become jaded, and we often take on the spiritual ill of cynicism. So it's important to create healthy boundaries in life, something wise people do and naïve ones don't. Trusting indiscriminately (such as believing that others have only pure motives) will leave you wounded, frustrated, and resentful.

BONUS INFORMATION: TWO-PART RESENTMENT

If you've been in church for a while, chances are you've heard numerous sermons on the importance of shedding resentment. It shrinks your soul and harms your body. One of my favorite descriptions of resentment is that it's like drinking a glass of poison while glaring at your enemy, hoping *he'll* die. Resentment is self-destructive.

But a message that you aren't likely to hear in church is how to *avoid feeling resentment* in the first place. This is too bad because it's a message many men need. It's no coincidence that CNGs are a resentful group. They experience more of it than your average Christian. So CNGs need to battle resentment on two fronts: dig up what's currently in their hearts, and stem future opportunities for resentment to take residence in their hearts. This is done by creating appropriate boundaries in life between you and others who are disrespectful toward you.

Think about the people you have resented. Be honest. Write down their names.

Do they have anything in common?
In what ways did they take advantage of you? Be specific.

Do you see a pattern in the behavior of these people?
Chances are, they weren't able to manipulate everyone around them because some people don't allow themselves to be manipulated.
How did those who resisted manipulation behave?

Were these people Christians?
How did their strong behavior affect their success in life?
What are some practical steps you can take today to build boundaries between you and those who are disrespectful toward you, helping you

become less resentful and harbor less sin in your heart in the future?

CNGs are also bitter because they envy more successful men. Who have you envied in the past and now?

How can you take the energy that you put into this kind of bitterness and turn it into admiration, the kind of energy that helps you create a better, more righteous life? (Hint, you may want to take the person out to lunch and explain to him that you admire his abilities and want him to share them with you.)

In what ways did you trust indiscriminately in the past? Without falling into the opposite trap of cynicism, how could you behave differently in the future? (Hint: naïveté and cynicism are opposite sides of the same scale. Being excessively simple and trusting is often a passive under-reaction to other people's actions. Cynicism is an overreaction.) Overcoming naïveté helps you become wise as a serpent. You become more like Jesus.

FEAR (FALSE EVIDENCE THAT APPEARS REAL)

As Rabbi Shmuley Boteach writes in his book *Face Your Fear: Living With Courage in an Age of Caution,* "We must accept that fear is not only harmful but evil, not only unhelpful but deeply destructive." And don't mistake fear for caution. Fear freezes people, while caution helps them to proceed with thoughtfulness. Think about a situation in which a person would have to choose between fearfulness and caution. Would that person's actions be different based on whether he was living out of fear or out of caution? What, if any difference, would you see?

Fear and passivity tend to affect people more in some areas of life than others. For example, some men can be assertive at work but passive at home.

Where are you most passive?

We are most passive where we are most fearful. What do you fear in this area?

Is this fear justified, or is it false evidence that appears real?

What can you do to help yourself distinguish between justified fear and false fear?

JESUS THE NAUGHTY NAZARENE

The dialogue between Jesus and Pilate as recorded in the Gospels is among the most penetrating and dramatic in history. Read at least one of these chapters to gain a greater sense of the interchange: Matthew 27, Mark 15, Luke 23, or John 18. We witness the collision between the values found in the Kingdom of God and in the Kingdom of Man.

Jesus tells Pilate the purpose of his driven life: to testify to the truth, and that all who respect the truth hear his voice. To which Pilate responds, "What is truth?" We condemn Pilate for asking this seemingly odd question, but when we look around and see how most live, we ask the same question, though not in so many words. Caring about truth often doesn't fortify our 401(k)s or lead to bigger homes and nicer cars. Twisting facts in our favor tends to get us ahead—at least for a season.

If I could choose one scene in the Bible where I could be a fly on the wall, it would be this moment. Whether I could bear its weight knowing the gruesome outcome, I don't know.

What surprises you about the exchange between Jesus and Pilate when you realize that Jesus was good, not nice?

What do you admire most in Jesus' behavior? Why?

Jesus is obstinate and argumentative before Pilate, which contradicts all notions that he was a meek and amiable presence. True, meek is a word synonymous with being yielding and submissive, but we fail to recognize what he was meek toward. He was yielding toward his Father's will, not the will of man. Being meek means you are to submit to the will of God, which often demands rugged behavior.

Though Jesus is resigned to fulfilling his redemptive mission of sacrificing his very life, *he does not resign himself to accepting the unjust and criminal manner by which his crucifixion takes place.* He remains the embodiment of truth.

Though he was cross-bound, Jesus does not go easily to his prophetic death. He's confrontational, willful—even disrespectful along the way. When asked to defend himself against trumped-up charges, he remains silent, which "astonished" Pilate. And when he does respond to the false accusation of naming himself the "King of the Jews," Jesus gives the rhetorical and disrespectful reply, "Is that your [Pilate's] own idea, or have others suggested it to you?" Jesus' response poignantly relays to Pilate that Jesus knew what kind of charade was being played against him. Jesus punctuates the fact that Pilate was a pawn in a deadly attempt at homicide. No one likes being accused of being a plaything of others. It is an insult. No wonder Pilate yelled.

Jesus was disrespectful before this brutal and cowardly authority figure. He was not robotic, dour, and colorless before the shadow of the crucifix, as he has been portrayed in too many movies and sermons.

Pilate heard about Jesus before meeting him, and when he saw him he was "greatly pleased" (Luke 23:8). He longed to see him "perform some miracle." Jesus made sure that his great pleasure didn't last long. Like most others, Pilate didn't understand Jesus, who did not behave like other men. There are times when I think that Pilate must have looked at Jesus the way we look at animals in a zoo.

Pilate tries one more time to get Jesus to admit to this false charge. Jesus refuses and shrewdly throws Pilate's sham words back at him.

Pilate: You are a king, then?

Jesus: King is your word. (John 18:37)

Create a list of the ways an ideal Christian man is supposed to behave regardless of how he is being treated. Then make a list of how Jesus responded to Pilate. Keep in mind that everything Jesus did or said was within his Father's will.

What would other Christians say if Christian men spoke the way Jesus did to an authority figure?

Why aren't Christian men (and women) allowed to behave like the real Jesus?

In what ways would you be freer and happier if you adopted this side of Jesus into your life?

How would you be better able to obtain the abundant life he wants for you?

Who do you think, if any, would come against you? Be specific.

JESUS THE BEARDED WOMAN

Jesus used shocking imagery to explain the mess we're in. Lopping off parts of our body that help us partake in sin is one of many that come to mind. He knew that shocking language and imagery can be effective mediums through which change occurs. And so it is with the title of this chapter and lesson. It should shock us into seeing him differently.

Jesus *is not* a bearded woman—someone around whom you pitch a tent and charge admission. But you wouldn't know this by how he is currently portrayed. The Jesus style, as it has been called, does include a nurturing component that is stereotypically thought of as feminine (but so does real masculinity, a fact addressed in Lessons 9 and 10). It also includes a rugged side that is well documented. It's this side that has been dropped from our current meditations about him, and the result is tragic, especially for passive Christian men.

These men, due to misconceptions learned as kids (we'll get to that in Lesson 4), already feel that it's wrong to exert their will. They think there's something deeply defective with them, so they treat their will (a composite of their wants and desires—which is a manifestation of who they are to the outside world) as if it's defective too. Many CNGs got this message from their homes, culture, and churches. They received a triple dose of feeling ashamed to be human and male. Crippling passivity is the result. Add to this mixture of shame a caricature of Jesus who was all sweet pickle and no jalapeño, and everyone suffers.

Others have complained about this problem and in various ways have tried to set the record straight, but with minimal success. They include Christian authors Stu Weber, Rick Bundschuh, Frederica Mathewes-Green, Philip Yancey, Charles Spurgeon, C. S. Lewis, and Dorothy L. Sayers, among others. But the belief that Jesus always minded his manners and never said a cross word still prevails. This shows that it's not a problem of interpretation, since the record is clear as to the personality Jesus possessed. It's an issue of preference. We prefer a soft Jesus to a tough one. We diminish our lives when we embrace this misunderstanding.

BONUS INFORMATION: DEHUMANIZED, DENATURED

What has happened to men in general and Christian men in particular hasn't been a feminization. We have been dehumanized and denatured. Being told to become bland and innocuous is, of course, not the same as being told to take on feminine characteristics. Women, often with the best of intentions, have also been encouraged to strip themselves of a compelling personality.

This dehumanizing message estranges us from our individuality, creativity, passion, and unique personality. This message isn't making us like women, who have been encouraged to undergo the same destructive and unbiblical transformation, but something other than truly human as made in the image of God. Our lives become dull, routine, and mechanical— the very characteristics that have haunted Christ's portrayal in most movies for far too long. As a result, we lose a vital sensitivity toward our lives and the lives of others. We are less able to enhance each other's lives because we have stripped ourselves of the ability to donate to one another a truly redemptive power.

Our denaturing has also come from the false message that passion is dangerous. King David has been held up to us as a cautionary tale in this regard. But nowhere in the Scriptures are we told to embrace its opposite of passionless and unemotional living. The last book of the Bible, Revelation, tells us that God would rather his creation be too hot or too cold instead of insipid "luke-warm" living (Revelation 3:16).

UNCHAINED SON: THE PARABLE OF JIM

Jesus told stories as a way of bypassing our many filters and prejudice. So I created a modern-day parable about what Jesus said and did in order to bypass today's prejudice toward him. I did this because many of us are too far gone. The Nice Nazarene is so much a part of our thinking that we can't comprehend another side to his personality. To many it feels blasphemous.

So I put Jesus' tough words and rugged behavior into the mouth and life of a guy named Jim. Read the Parable of Jim in chapter 2. If you're in a group, have someone read it out loud.

- In what ways does it feel wrong to think of Jesus this way?
- Why would it feel wrong to think about him this way when the Bible records these actions?
- There's humor in this parable, which is an effective tool for helping truth to get past our prejudices by showing how some things in life don't add up. The real Jesus and the one we read about in Christian books and hear on Christian radio and in church seem like two different people.
- Why is this?
- What part of the Parable of Jim sticks in your mind (or your throat) the most? Why?

○ Compare the Parable of Jim—the words and actions of Jesus—to how the ideal Christian man is expected to behave. Make a list. On the right put down what you know about Jesus as found in this parable.

What qualities does he possess?

Now look at the list you made in Lesson 1 about what qualities a Christian man should possess.

If these lists are different, ask yourself why.

Jesus shocked and offended people. Why do we consider this sinful behavior?

Name a time when you shocked and offended others while testifying to the truth.

Name a man you know who emulates the qualities found in this parable (authenticity, boldness, sarcasm/exaggeration, and so on).

Is it easier for you to name a woman?

If a guy like Jim went to your church, where would he fit in, if at all?

WARNING

The Parable of Jim is concentrated toughness. You don't want to follow this Jesus because he's unbalanced by other parts of his personality. It would be dangerous to try to emulate only this side of Jesus, just as it is equally dangerous to emulate only a Nice Jesus. The Good Guy Rebellion is about a balanced view of Jesus, which will give us a balanced and healthier approach toward life.

 **GOOD GUY WORKOUT**
A Whole Other Gospel

This section, "A Whole Other Gospel," shows how alive the Gospels become when we release Jesus from his Nice Guy buttoned-down persona. It includes words and phrases that show the tougher and more rugged side of the world in which Jesus walked. You get my list, but you should make your own. This way it becomes part of your study and experience. Get out that journal of yours and keep an ongoing list of these words. It helps to jot down the name of the book and the chapter.

 How come these words didn't pop out before?

SETTING THE RECORD STRAIGHT

This section takes the Nice Guy Jesus misconception even deeper to show just how "non-Christian" Jesus' behavior really was. It shows the mental gyrations and dishonesty we are forced to keep alive in order to keep Jesus tame. Atop this list is the idea that he disapproved of the consumption of wine. This is remarkable since Jesus could have chosen a different setting to unveil his first recorded miracle that carried the additional significance of revealing "his glory, and his disciples put their faith in him."

WARNING

Like many others, I have read accounts of possession in Scripture and wondered why I don't see this kind of weirdness today. But then I think of the people I've known who were addicted to drugs and alcohol. These addictions are a form of possession. You see evil's fingerprints on them. Destruction gives the game away.

A glass of wine does not make a drunkard out of everyone. But it can out of some. Alcoholism is nothing to smile about. It has ruined countless lives, and what I've written here is not an excuse to be a lush. It has a genetic component that tends to run in families. If you think this genetic predisposition might include you, be very careful. It's possible that partaking in wine or other forms of alcohol is off limits to you.

If you're unsure if alcoholism runs in your family, find out. Ask someone in your family or someone who is close to your family. Ask people who are known for telling the truth, warts and all. Dig deep if you have to. This is part of being wise as a serpent.

If you find out that alcoholism is part of your family's history, talk to someone who overcame it. Most recovering alcoholics are more than happy to share their story. Chances are, you'll learn a lot about suffering, grief, freedom, and redemption.

I helped someone I love seek treatment for alcoholism. I told her that many of our fears are illusions. They possess only assumed power, not real power. They are the stuff of our imagination that runs away when we confront them.

Helping this woman is among the proudest moments of my life. She's two years clean and sober—and counting.

DOES THIS MAKE YOU CRINGE?

Now to an essential point. As previously mentioned, Jesus tells us to be "wise as serpents and harmless as doves" (Matthew 10:16 NKJV). The word *phronimos*, where we get the word for wise, can also be translated as "cunning" and "shrewd." Jesus goes on to tell those who follow him, who take up the redemptive work of God, to be wary of those who attempt to persecute them. Doesn't sound like he wants us to be naïve and fatalistic to the world around us, does it?

Think about the ideal Christian man again. Is he supposed to be cunning and shrewd? Does this make you uneasy? If so, why?

Are you capable of dealing with others in a clever manner, possessing intelligence, insight, and sound judgment? Do you behave with skillful ingenuity? Would you characterize such behavior as passive or proactive?

How would your life change if you were more clever, original, and effective, which is the definition of ingenious, which is related to shrewdness?

Chances are, you've heard many sermons on what it means to be innocent as a dove.

But have you heard sermons on how to be wise as a serpent?

If not, why, since Jesus never said one component was more important than the other?

If there is an imbalance here, what does it tell you about the current state of many churches?

What does this tell you about your life?

PAUL AND STEPHEN: NO "NICE" GUYS

The Scriptures are packed with un-nice guy behavior, if only we get past our prejudices to see them. And contrary to what we may think, love causes us to be confrontational at times (Proverbs 27:5).

When was the last time you confronted someone due to loving concern? How did it go?

Think about the confrontational moments in your life. Chances are, you experienced the fire-breathing kind that destroys and never creates a better life. Journal the moments that come to mind.

Who confronted you, and how did they handle your emotions? Did they attack you, or was their demeanor caring and loving?

What was the result?

How is passion confused for anger?

A WORD ON CONFRONTATION

Most have received unsolicited advice about their lives from others. Not a pleasant experience. Human nature being what it is, uninvited criticism doesn't sit well. Our ears often close pretty quickly, even if these words contain truth and healing.

Remember that the goal of your confrontation isn't to "nail" someone for his or her behavior. The Good Guy Rebellion creates redemptive forces for good with the goal of making a bad situation better.

Address people's behavior and don't condemn their personhood. Point out what their behavior is doing to them and what it's doing to those close to them. Show concern, not condemnation.

SPECIAL CARE WITH KIDS

For some reason we sometimes don't believe kids deserve this level of respect when confronted. Remember that rules without relationship lead to rebellion with kids. When confronting their behavior, leave them with the impression that you are doing so not because you have nothing better to do, but because you are concerned for their well-being. You are struggling to help them create a better life for themselves. Leave them with the solid understanding that you are in their corner. You have their back.

LISTEN TO PHILEMON

Read Paul's letter to Philemon. It's only a page. Note Paul's craftiness. Write these moments down. Then ask yourself: *Have I been crafty on behalf of another person?* If not, why not?

Does it feel wrong to be crafty while being a redemptive force for good? If so, why would it feel wrong for you but not for the apostle Paul?

Paul wrote to the Galatians, "Why don't these agitators [Jews who became Christian but wanted to retain Jewish codes of conduct], obsessive as they are about circumcision, go all the way and castrate themselves!" (Galatians 5:12 THE MESSAGE).

Do you think it's wrong for you to use such powerful language when confronting false beliefs about God?

Have you ever used such language?

Why or why not?

Have you heard a Christian man speak in this manner?

If so, how did you feel, and what does this feeling tell you about yourself?

What did others do?

DON'T GET CARRIED AWAY, STEPHEN

Stephen, "filled with the Holy Spirit," we're told in the book of Acts, grew combative with his audience. He tongue-lashed them, and they later murdered him.

Have you been told that God's Holy Spirit can lead you into intense confrontation as it did with Stephen?

How does this make you feel and think about God?

We often talk about the Holy Spirit's power in our life. Think about the words that are synonymous with power. This chapter lists the words vitality, intensity, emotional expression, will, force, action, and impetus. There are more.

Write down in your journal other words that represent power; specifically, human traits that relate to powerful people. (Note: Power is neither good nor bad. *How* it's used dictates its ability to help or hurt. So forget about the dark side of power for now. The Good Guy Rebellion is about creating good works, so write down traits of powerful people who do good.)

How many of these traits are men in general and Christian men in particular encouraged to exercise? For example, how many Christian men (other than worship leaders) do you know who express their emotions powerfully? Are Christian men told to be this way, or stoic?

The Bible says that the righteous are as bold as lions (Proverbs 28:1). How many bold Christian men do you know? Write down their names. More importantly, what makes them bold? Be specific.

UNCHAINED FATHER

Let's switch now to our understanding of God the Father. In the Old Testament, God commits warfare on behalf of dependent Israel and battles against rebellious Israel. The name Israel means "He who wrestles with God."

Do you think it's "Christian" to wrestle with God? How can wrestling with God be an expression of intimacy?

What issue would you most like to wrestle with him about? Be specific.

When Eugene Peterson translated the Psalms into contemporary language, he concluded that about 70 percent were complaints and lamentations to God. Yet the ideal Christian man isn't supposed to complain about much of anything—including injustice.

How is it not "Christian" to complain to God?

Think for a moment if God were nice instead of good. We would be the recipients of pleasant platitudes, not life-giving wisdom and love, because sometimes such information makes us uncomfortable. Discomfort is the enemy of all things nice. Think about a nice drug treatment program. What would be the success rate if people were told that tomorrow will be a brighter day, but they were not given the insight and confrontation necessary to change destructive thinking?

Why do we think God the Father, Son, and Holy Spirit are always nice and amiable when such character wouldn't make them redemptive forces but powerless and naïve instead?

It's clear that they weren't nice. So why do we think we have to be nice all the time?

"BLESSED SARCASM"

Jesus' sarcasm woke me up unlike anything else, because in my mind I held a weak equation: Jesus was a Nice Guy. Therefore, I should be too.

But Nice Guys don't do sarcasm. It's off limits to Christian men. To some it may well feel sinful because it goes against our unofficial church motto, "If you don't have anything nice to say, don't say it at all" (The Gospel According to Ms. Manners 1:1).

But Jesus was sarcastic, which blows the lid off the belief that he was a nice guy. And as explained in this chapter, our theology is shipwrecked if we refuse to acknowledge this.

Why do we refuse to think Jesus used redemptive humor when the best teachers use humor? Do we think it detracts from his divinity? If so, why do we think this when it's clear that his Father used sarcasm when relating to Job?

Humor, as Jesus showed us, can be a very serious thing. I believe that humorless people possess a spiritual rigidity and deficiency: an inability to recognize and appreciate irony, around which much of our spiritual lives revolve (more on that later). As a result, I won't let such people into my inner circle of influence.

Think about the humorless people in your life. How do they live?

Do you want to be more or less like them? Why?

CAUTION: SARCASM

Jesus reserved his sarcasm for the arrogant, powerful, hypocritical, and dangerous.

Notice how Jesus didn't unleash sarcasm upon children or the downtrodden. Neither should we.

Like a lot of CNGs, I received sarcasm as a child. It's unfair and abusive because kids don't have the mental capacity to defend themselves against it.

Sarcasm can also be a hiding place for people who are too fearful to tell others what they really think. (This certainly wasn't the case with Jesus.) So be sure that if you use sarcasm, you aren't doing so due to cowardly inclinations.

THE RESULT OF FALSE BELIEF: WEAK LIVING

All this "nice" living, the result of false beliefs, weakens us. For many Christian men, attending men's conferences and reading books aimed at Christian men has resulted in an unbalanced life. After living by an incomplete message and after the emotional highs wear off, many Christian men still feel guilty for being male, for having a will, and they think it's wrong to behave like the real Jesus.

It's bad enough that those who claim to know the Living God are often weaker than those who don't. But others suffer due to our weakness. Wives, children, the weak and timid, the poor and the oppressed go without our donations and blessings of strength, support, and protection.

Like my caller Dan, have you been told that it's a sin to stand up for yourself to physical and verbal bullies?

Why is it damaging to tell your children that it's wrong to stand up for themselves?

Why do we believe that we should allow ourselves to be abused when Jesus did not literally turn his cheek so an abusive guard could slap him on the other side of his face? (See John 18.)

When Jesus said to no longer seek revenge against another (i.e., an eye for an eye), he was telling us not to return evil for evil.

Why do we believe that self-defense is evil, especially when we are made in God's image, which gives us intrinsic worth?

Where did we get these false beliefs?

OTHER EARNEST BUT DAMAGING CHURCH MESSAGES TO MEN

Chapter 3 describes the predicament men discover at church. Many are asked to check their masculinity at the door, among other problems. Men sense this and stay away. This lesson, based on the same chapter, takes you through the reasons why this problem exists, and it suggests the issues that must change in order for men to *want* to go to church and *want* to be at home.

TOUGH MEDICINE

Many people, both conservative and liberal, look back on the sexual revolution of the 1960s with varying levels of regret. Much damage was done to society, especially to children, as seen in rising crime and poverty rates due to out of wedlock births. Numerous children grew up without the multi-faceted benefit of fathers in their home, making life more difficult, as described in chapter 7.

This movement handed society the greatest period of gender

confusion in modern time. The church was one of the few organizations to fight back. It prescribed a medicine with an unintended side effect. It told men to take their domestic responsibilities more seriously since the family unit was falling apart. Unfortunately, they were told to adopt a feminine understanding of domesticity. This unintentional side effect softened and frustrated men.

Before we explore the specifics of this softening, it's important to acknowledge that the feminist movement of the 1960s and '70s did not take place in a vacuum. Women have been treated poorly. Even conservatives such as Dr. James Dobson remember how poorly women were treated in the workplace. I list a few examples that I witnessed, beginning on page fifty.

Think for a moment about the prejudice you have seen against women. Write these incidents down, then ask yourself:

Why would a man feel compelled to denigrate a woman in the first place?

How would such a person be trustworthy in other areas of life?

What will you say or do the next time someone makes derogatory statements about women?

Good Guy Workout

Watch a rerun of *All in the Family*. Listen to the laughs Archie Bunker gets when looking down on women. Do you think such punch lines would be tolerated today?

Now compare Hollywood's treatment of women then to how men are treated in today's sitcoms. *Everybody Loves Raymond* is a painful example of how fathers are often portrayed. Ray, the main character, is funny but in a bumbling and foolish way. He can never seem to get his act together, and his wife, Debra, is always bailing him out.

○ Do you think this low view of men will be funny twenty years from now?

o Make a list of smart and capable men and fathers on television today. Now make a list of smart and capable women and mothers. Compare the lists. Which is longer? Any idea why? Tell someone about the prejudice you see against men in the popular media, and show concern for what this is telling boys and young men.

HOME ECONOMICS 101

A study from the University of Virginia found that the wives of conservative evangelical husbands rank them higher than other U.S. men in most every category when it comes to domestic responsibilities and overall happiness. Though these wives are pleased with their husbands, no such survey supports the general happiness of conservative evangelical men. This is because they are expected to behave at home in accordance to feminine codes and rules.

For example: think about your home. If you're not married, think about the homes of married men you know. Do they have a say in how it is decorated?

If he does repairs, are they seen as acts of love toward his family?

Most likely they are not, though the work that women traditionally perform at home is thought of in this light.

Why the double standard?

Is your home, or the homes of other men you know, receptive to roughhousing and vigorous debate?

Are men allowed to be loud?

Are robust opinions nurtured or quieted?

Are children allowed to get messy?

Are boys allowed to take physical risks even with the potential for minor injury?

When boys gather at your home, are they encouraged only to play "non-violent" games as defined by women?

Does the home not have a dog, though the kids have wanted one for years?

Are boys criticized for expressing their individuality and are girls congratulated for homogenizing?

Are boys supposed to be nice and pleasant all the time, even when bothered or bullied?

Are men and boys allowed to get angry? Are they allowed to cry?

Are men told they don't load the dishwasher "right"? What would a man be called if he criticized how his wife mowed the lawn or organized a tool bench?

Who controls the social calendar in your home? (Hint: statistically it's not the guy.) Husbands complain that their friends and family tend to slip off this calendar that's controlled by wives, making it difficult to get together with them.

Is this an abuse of power?

What would a man be called if he limited his wife's time with her friends and family?

The point to all these questions? They are designed to discern if your home is dominated by feminine sensibilities, rules, and codes. If so, encourage her to share her power justly.

If you realize that this is the case in your home, *do not get angry with your wife*. Getting upset about this fact is like getting upset about the weather. It's the way things are, but it doesn't mean it has to stay this way.

Again, these questions aren't asked in order to point a finger at the wonderful women in our lives. My wife is my best friend, my most trusted advisor. We have talked about how homes in general are dominated by a feminine spirit, and I suggest you do the same.

We have talked about how if men are rightly expected to be more domestic (compared with years past), then men should be allowed to help define the mood, tone, and philosophy of their home. This will help lead to *genuine* domestic bliss as opposed to the fake kind we have now where men just keep their mouths shut and escape through convenient hobbies, an underreported form of passive-aggressive behavior.

Discuss how you can make your home a mixture of male and female awareness. Create a list. Even Martha Stewart might say, "That's a good thing."

NEW SPIRITUAL ORDER: WOMEN ARE MORE SPIRITUAL

A myth floated by our churches, and our culture is that women are more moral and spiritual than men. This is one reason why the mystical religion of Kabbalah is gaining popularity. It asserts the supremacy of the feminine over the masculine.

There is no better time to see how this prejudice plays out than during Mother's Day and Father's Day, especially at church.

Writes one blogger:

> At my old Finnish "Lutheran" church in Upper Michigan, the pastor there would praise and nearly worship wives and mothers of the congregation on Mother's Day.
> But then came Father's Day.
> I dreaded it. He had all of the husbands get down on our knees in front of our wives to beg their forgiveness in prayer for falling so short in being lousy fathers and dads. He'd yell at us in the sermon, saying something like our kids are going to hell because of the crummy jobs that we were doing. . . .

Another frustrated reader:

> For years I have heard Mother's Day sermons that praise how virtuous women are, followed a month later with Father's Day sermons that berate Christian men for not doing their job, telling them

they need to be "nicer" guys. Paul said that as we progress in our faith, we need to move from spiritual milk to meat, but it would seem that some pastors are handing out a lot of baloney instead of the steak that God intended for men to receive.

Have you ever heard in church that women are more moral and spiritual than men? Many CNGs have. It's usually said with a lot of confidence and sometimes charisma. It sounds so plausible given how women outnumber men in all forms of Christianity, with the possible exception of Eastern Orthodox.

It's time to do some Bible sleuthing.

Where does it say in the Bible that women are more moral and spiritual than men? (Hint: nowhere. I thought I'd save you some time.)

Since this belief is found nowhere in the Bible, we are free to ask questions regarding the motives of such preachers. What do you think motivates them to say this?

Think of the ramifications of saying one gender is more moral and spiritual than another. It would make sense that this gender would occupy all areas of leadership and that others must adopt their opinions and views about life in general. This would equate to gender tyranny.

In what ways is a minister who elevates women in this way sinning against an entire gender?

If this describes your minister or church, how can you help reform your church so it will halt its prejudice toward men? (Hint: Don't try to do it alone. There is strength in numbers.)

HUSBAND'S TO BLAME

Many Christian guys have been told that if their marriage is bad for most any reason, it's their fault and their responsibility to fix it. This also bears false witness against an entire gender. It's a sin, and Christian men (some of whom have left the church over this issue) are owed a massive group apology.

Where does it say in the Bible that husbands alone are responsible for the well-being of their marriage?

In what ways is it unfair and destructive to blame a man for all of his marriage problems?

SACRIFICE EVERYTHING. EXPECT NOTHING.

Christian men have been told to sacrifice themselves for their wives and children and expect nothing in return for their sacrifice. This has been explained as being "Christlike."

Why have we been told it's wrong to expect something in return for our hard work and sacrifice, especially when the Bible tells us not to withhold compensation for work done (Deuteronomy 25:4)?

In what ways would a husband become unattractive to his wife if he decided to give up his interests and passions in order to constantly serve his wife?

What do you think this message does to a man's desire to go to church?

C. S. LEWIS ON ABANDONING OUR LIKES AND SIMPLE PLEASURES

C. S. Lewis's *Screwtape Letters* is a collection of fictitious letters from a senior demonic henchman to a subordinate, instructing him on how to steal a person's faith and suck the life out of us humans in other ways, leaving us limp and lifeless. Sadly, the strategy outlined in this letter— mentioning a man's likes and simple pleasures, which they are then told to discard—is employed by parts of the church.

The deepest likings and impulses of any man are the raw

material, the starting-point, with which the Enemy [God] has furnished him. To get him away from those is therefore always a point gained. . . . I myself would carry this very far. I would make it a rule to eradicate from my patient [the human this henchman is tormenting] any strong personal taste which is not actually a sin, even if it is something quite trivial such as . . . collecting stamps or drinking cocoa. . . . There is a sort of innocence and humility and self-forgetfulness about them which I distrust. The man who truly and disinterestedly enjoys any one thing in the world, for its own sake, and without caring two-pence what other people say about it, is by that very fact forearmed against some of our subtlest modes of attack.

GOING DEEPER

As Dr. Laura points out in her bestselling book *The Proper Care & Feeding of Husbands,* generations of women have grown up suspicious of men and with a troubling low level of respect for men. Some wives aren't inclined to respect their husband's sacrifices—regardless of what some ministers preach. Their husbands are resentful and they may leave such women for those who have a more mature understanding of men.

In such a situation, where do you think the sin began: with the divorce or with the disrespectful treatment?

In what ways would it be better to go to the root of the problem and help such women become more respectful?

Is it common for women as a whole to be corrected at church? If not, why?

AMERICA'S FEMINIZED FAITH

The section beginning on page sixty-one of *No More Christian Nice Guy,* "Taking Ephesians Too Far," lists some of the more stomach-churning examples from recent history of how the real Jesus has been portrayed as history's Nicest Guy. Horace Bushnell, a popular figure of his time, chose to describe Jesus as a flower, a man who was a "perfectly harmless being, actuated by no destructive passions, gentle to inferior, doing ill or injury to no one." According to Bushnell, Jesus embodied the "passive virtues."

Bushnell's characterization falls apart when cross-examined with the gospel facts. Still, he was an influential theologian in his time and his views were widely accepted.

It's easy to look into history and see where we went wrong. But let's look at how Jesus is portrayed today in church, popular culture, and places where Christian books and related products are sold.

Re-read the parable of Jim on page thirty, then think about places where Christian books and images are held. What do you notice?

If you possess artistic ability, consider creating more accurate imagery yourself.

GOOD GUY REBELLION ROLL CALL

Fortunately for me, the only church I've been involved with has a balanced view of Jesus. But it doesn't require a great leap to know that this view is out there. It's too bad that a lot of men are taught only the meek, mild, turn-the-other-cheek Jesus. . . . We forget about Joshua, Daniel, Jacob, Peter, and Paul. The first time I read Daniel I realized that what we believe in is not only worth fighting for, but it is worth dying for. I was reading Acts yesterday and realized that if Peter and Paul didn't have the courage to do what they did in the face of unrelenting persecution, the Gospel might not have been spread.

—Scott

Problems With Paradox

Paradox is a statement, proposition, or situation that seems to be absurd or contradictory, but in fact is or may be true. Much of our spiritual lives revolve around this concept, so the sooner we understand it and embrace it the better off we'll be.

For various reasons we have a hard time understanding how Jesus could be both gentle and tough. We think this kind of living is contradictory, that somehow our tough behavior wipes away the gentle acts we commit.

Think about your understanding of love.

Write down words, phrases, and actions that you associate with love. Next to these statements, when possible, write down examples found in the Bible.

Does your list include more sentimental and romantic examples of love? This is great and valuable. Romance is one reason I got married and why I'm happily married. And this makes sense because we live during a pretty sentimental age.

But there is another side to love, one that's tougher, rugged—a side that lasts longer.

I'd like to point out two things Jesus did that demonstrate love's full spectrum: when he corrected his followers from stopping the children from coming to him, and when he picked up a whip in the temple and turned over tables.

Do you think the latter is an act of love? If not, consider this: he confronted people making sordid gain off of religion because he wanted to stop them from abusing the people he loved. It was also an act of love on behalf of his Father. The temple was his home. By confronting the corruption in his Father's house, he was showing love to his Father.

Look for other examples from the Bible, history in general, and your own life, where rugged behavior was actually loving behavior.

Jesus the Naughty Nazarene

"You have a fine way of rejecting the commandment of God." Jesus said this to the Pharisees (Mark 7:9 ESV).

Think about it. Do we really think Jesus complimented an entire group for ignoring God's commands? We do when we refuse to acknowledge that Jesus used sarcasm.

So the next time you ask yourself WWJD, are you open to the possibility that it might include a sarcastic response?

GOOD GUY REBELLION ROLL CALL

Finally! Coughlin poses the question I've wondered about for years . . . Why aren't Christians more willing to use and enjoy humor—especially sarcasm? In answering his own question, Coughlin says . . . "A satirist needs the guts to stand up in public, point at the actions of someone else, and loudly say 'WRONG!' " Jeez . . . sounds like what prophets did and do. Jeez . . . sounds like what Jesus did, and dare we say would enjoy doing today?! Too bad more guys value being "nice" over speaking what God, by the power of His Holy Moly Spirit, has put into their renewed minds.

I see this seeming obtuse proposition . . . as a true "crux of what's the matter" with Christian men who are mistakenly trying to fly below the radar of what today's culture/cosmos has produced . . . namely guys who are afraid to speak their minds. It's just that simple. Fear shuts your mouth up and shuts your heart and spirit down.

On the other hand . . . a little sarcasm and satire creates a crack, an opening, a leverage point for "those who have ears to hear," to quote one of the greatest "stand-up performers" of all time. Oh yeah . . . He still likes to get up on the stage. Read

Coughlin's book and you just might find yourself being His mouth-piece in an unexpected manner . . . like speaking the truth in love and humor . . . something this world is hungry for!
—Mike

CHILDHOOD, WHERE WE LEARNED TO LIVE SMALL

The scars left from the child's defeat in the fight against irrational authority are to be found at the bottom of every neurosis.
—Erich Fromm, social philosopher and psychoanalyst

Nice Guys aren't born excessively passive, fearful, and emotionless. Something profound happened to them, usually as boys, that caused them to live by the following motto: "If I live small, my troubles will be few."

Nice Guys are made, not born. They should not be mistaken for reserved men who, with time, let their will be known. Nice Guys relinquish and smother their will. They believe that what they think, feel, and do doesn't matter, and therefore this world doesn't need them. The feel as if they are an extra toy pumped out on an assembly line with no intrinsic value, purpose, or mission in life. They look to others to assign them value, a dangerous expectation under any circumstance. Such men feel inside like a kind of leftover, a child of an indifferent god.

Spiritual writer Donald Miller, author of the bestselling *Blue Like Jazz*, struggled with this same problem, the result of growing up without a dad around. Being a boy without a father put a hole inside Miller—a hole numerous CNGs possess and must feel and understand before a healing can begin. He writes in *To Own a Dragon: Reflections on Growing Up Without a Father,* "To me, life was something you had to stumble through alone. It wasn't something you enjoyed or conquered, it was something that happened to you, and you didn't have a whole lot to say about the way it turned out. . . . I wondered if some of the confusing emotions I was feeling weren't a kind of suspended adolesence from which the presence of an older man might have delivered me."

CNGs think they don't matter and that their choices in life don't make much of a difference. As a result, they lay down the sword of their will, usually due to being shamed, confused, or condemned by one or more important adult figures in their childhood who made them feel powerless and helpless. This thinking has more to do with the philosophy of fatalism, the belief that man cannot influence his destiny by exercising his will, than authentic Christianity. He feels rudderless but pretends that he doesn't. CNGs bring this thinking into adult life, often undetected. This false view of life haunts them in all major areas of life. This lesson, based on chapter 4, helps you understand how this condition was born and how to exhume it from your life.

This is one of the more powerful lessons in this Study Guide. Much of the CNG problem revolves around the difficulties men had as kids, and how they have mishandled and misunderstood these difficulties.

Though the majority of the fear-causing events took place in childhood, this doesn't mean that all do. As my conversation with a struggling CNG who was sexually assaulted in a Greek prison as a teenager shows, trauma during other periods of life create the same damaging lifestyle.

"My wife tells me I'm fearful and too passive sometimes," he confided in me, tears in his eyes. This tall, muscular, and handsome man told me he wasn't always so prone to submit and obey without resistance. *No More Christian Nice Guy,* especially chapter 4, showed him what this experience did to him. He felt relief and hope for the first time in decades. It's remarkable the pain we carry inside, and how looks are so deceiving.

Some men think that exploring these issues isn't important, it's a waste of time or un-Christian somehow. I know such men. I used to be one. Without exception, they cover their fear of emotions with weak excuses. Don't be one of them. Don't let convenient arguments stop you from an abundant life, from being more like Jesus, who was not owned by shame, fear, and a life-numbing refusal to feel life to its fullest.

NOWHERE TO HIDE

Beginning on page seventy, I describe what fundamental episodes of my life were like as a boy at the hands of a troubled and abusive mother. Christian Nice Guys tell me that this description of physical and emotional abuse stirred their memories of similar treatment. It started them on the path toward additional insight about their inner lives. And with this insight can come powerful healing.

GOOD GUY WORKOUT

If by yourself, read the "Nowhere to Hide" section, keeping track of your feelings. Write them down. Just a word like "sad" will work. Then search your memory for similar incidents in your own life. If your thoughts come too quickly, jot down a phrase or even a word that encapsulates the moment for you. This is the essential raw material that will help you realize that passive people are made, not born. Pain, properly handled, is a conduit toward a better life. It can help you see life more clearly, blazing a trail for greater insight and healing.

If in a group, have someone read the section aloud, but still keep track of your feelings. Write down moments that were similar in your own life. Share these moments with the group. (Note to group leaders: You'll want to remind everyone that what's said in your group stays in your group. You will likely see how some issues will go deeper with some men than others. Some of what they say and do may be extraordinary and require extraordinary insight. If this happens, encourage such men to speak with a trained counselor in your area.)

BONUS INFORMATION: THE GOOD SIDE OF SADNESS

Some guys fear emotions. And so they do their best to keep them submerged. When they do show deep emotion, some feel that it's a sign of weakness. That's a total lie.

There's a profound religious component to this as well. For some misguided reason, we believe that being Christian means not showing emotions. The record is clear on this point: Jesus showed more emotion, not less, than those around him. And he said to emulate his behavior. Without emotions, we become caricatures. We don't really live.

If you feel sadness during this lesson, celebrate! It means the CNG problem is not as bad as it could be. It means your emotional life is still active. If you don't feel sadness after reading about the pain of another, then the CNG problem is worse for you. That's all right. It just means you have some more ground to cover. You are never without hope.

HELP FOR MINISTERS

We spend a lot of time in church talking about the spiritual ill of pride and arrogance, of thinking too much about ourselves. But I've never heard a sermon about the sin and spiritual sickness of self-loathing, of thinking too little about ourselves. Ministers, millions of men (and women) need your help.

Given what you now know about the CNG problem, what are ways you can incorporate these insights into your upcoming sermons?

How can you explain to your congregation that thinking too much and too little about yourself are both wrong?

(Note: We're all ministers, though some have larger platforms than others. We're all called to lead redemptive lives, which requires intelligent leadership. Part of leadership is defining reality for others.)

SHAME VELCRO

There's an odd phenomenon that haunts CNGs who had abusive and/ or neglectful childhoods. They are attracted to individuals and groups that are abusive too. Nowhere is this more insidious than in church. This is why I write: *People with troubled pasts should avoid churches that make them feel ashamed for being human.* Such unintentional treatment is spiritual abuse.

Here's a checklist to help recognize a church that spiritually abuses its people.

1. Does your church often denounce other churches from the pulpit for not being truly "Christian"?
2. Are criticisms about the church characterized as "attacks from Satan"?
3. Do leaders portray themselves as being more spiritual and morally superior to you because they are part of "God's anointed"?
4. Are people pressured to attend all church functions?
5. Do the leaders claim to have special insight into Scripture that others don't possess—therefore their actions should never be questioned?
6. Are people manipulated through guilt, intimidation, and discipline that's carried out publicly?
7. Do you feel worthless and undeserving of human dignity after sermons?
8. Do people drop other activities (school) and responsibilities

(commitment to spouse and children) in order to be at church to "work for the Lord"?

9. Is leaving such a church accompanied with warnings of divine judgment where "blessings" from leadership will be withheld?

10. Has someone you trust and respect warned you about the church you attend?

If you attended such a church and no longer do, what do you think this experience did to you? For example, are you more or less trusting of authority figures? Did your appreciation for human dignity increase or decrease? Do you still feel angry and abused? What have you done with these inner changes, if anything?

Would you have been better off not going to church at all? Why or why not?

Like Philip Yancey did, you will eventually need to forgive an abusive church the way you will need to forgive abusive or neglectful parents.

You may not know it right now, but there are churches that don't treat people this way. The grace you receive from these better churches may feel strange and wrong at first (it did for me), but hang in there. Freedom from continual condemnation is coming. Your spirit and your life will grow in unforeseen ways.

GOING DEEPER

What do you think being made in God's image really means?

For example, can someone be the bearer of God's image and be worthless at the same time?

Why or why not?

OUR UNOFFICIAL MOTTO

A Nice Guy believes *If I live small, my troubles will be few.* This is due primarily to a fear of conflict.

How does living small make life worse? (Hint: think about what it does with your relationship with God, home life, work life.)

How does a life defined by faith require risk?

How did Jesus handle conflict?

What effect does fear have on your courage and boldness?

PREJUDICE AGAINST COUNSELING

We often see two extreme and dangerous responses to childhood trauma. One is to pretend that it didn't happen. And when we reluctantly acknowledge that it did happen, we pretend that we are robots, not human. We naïvely conclude that it didn't really influence us.

The other response is to embrace the trauma but not its cure. Some people use childhood difficulties as excuses for weak and selfish living and take up an unofficial quest to make other people pay for the injustices done to them.

Most passive CNGs go the nothing-happened-to-me route, and some combine it with a prejudice against counseling (which is unfortunate since proper counseling is another avenue for seeking wisdom higher than their own, something the Bible encourages us to do. For many CNGs, it's part of being wise as a serpent).

Another argument goes like this: Everything you need to know in life is found in the Bible, so there's no need to go to any person for additional help. Interesting. Let's think about that for a second. Say you want to change jobs, or the place you work goes under. Either way, you need to find another job. Often this includes additional training and learning. According to the Bible-only argument, you have no need for additional schooling. All you need to do is read your Bible. Imagine an accountant who looks to the Bible alone to become an electrician or cardiologist? Would you hire him?

The Bible admonishes us to seek wisdom higher than our own, to seek wise counsel. This comes from God and wiser people. Why do we think it's okay to seek greater insight when it comes to making money, but wrong when it comes to renewing our minds, which leads to better lives and less sin?

Here's another prejudice. It is true that some bonehead ideas have been floated in the name of psychology. Christians opposed to counseling often point to this fact to bolster their argument that the entire field is not just foolish but dangerous. But the same baby-with-the-bath-water argument can be applied to seeing your neighborhood doctor. There was a time when physicians leaked blood out of sick patients, thinking their blood was the source of their illness. This led to many deaths. The history of medicine is replete with dangerous assumptions and oversights. Yet most everyone still seeks medical help. Why the double standard?

BONUS INFORMATION: INSIGHT INTO ABUSERS

Abusive people should never be mistaken for courageous people. Though both may use physical and verbal force against another, abusive people usually enter battles when assured of victory. And they fight only for their own ego and appetites. Courageous people fight on behalf of something bigger than themselves, and they fight whether assured of victory or not.

Abusers are gifted at judging power balances and shifts. They are small and pitiful in this regard. They know that the world of power can be divided into real and assumed power. Real power is the kind prison guards possess. They have the actual power to make life miserable for another. (Though as Holocaust survivor Viktor Frankl explains, they do not have the power to take your dignity if you don't let them.)

Most people don't have this kind of power; abusers know how to appear *as if* they possess power. They will often do this by withholding something you think you need from them, namely their approval. They sense your need to please everyone around you, and they exploit this nice-guy weakness. The amount of exploitation is often the result of the distance between their cunning and your naïveté.

List the abusive people in your life when you were a child.

What did they do to you?

Why were they able to do it?

Now list the abusive people in your life now.

What are they doing to you?

What assumed power do they claim to possess? (For example, abusive bosses will make it appear as if they are the only game in town, as if there are no *Help Wanted* ads posted anywhere. This is not an accident.)

What are they claiming to withhold from you?

Do you really need it? (Remember: FEAR is often False Evidence that Appears Real.)

GOOD GUY WORKOUT

Because CNGs are usually harder on themselves than other people (CNGs are adept at dismissing their own thoughts and feelings too easily), I want you to envision a boy you care about undergoing the kinds of problems you had as a boy. Chances are, you would show sympathy for such a kid. You would see pretty clearly how such treatment messes up his life. You would tell him he's valuable.

Why, then, do you think that you aren't valuable?

Who are the people who made you feel most valuable as a kid?

How did these people behave?

Now apply this same behavior to yourself.

JESUS THE NAUGHTY NAZARENE

"You hypocrites, why are you trying to trap me?" (Matthew 22:18). Jesus said this to the Pharisees, who tried to trap him regarding the issue of a Roman poll tax, which was fiercely resented by patriotic Jews as a symbol of their political subjection.

This was a trap because some twenty-five years previously, another man from Galilee, Judas, led a major revolt against this tax (Acts 5:37). The similarity with Jesus was great. If the Pharisees could get Jesus to speak against the tax, they would have damaging information against him before Roman authorities.

By getting the Pharisees to produce a denarius coin, Jesus exposes their hypocrisy. The coin boasted the portrait of the emperor with the inscription "Son of God." No patriotic Jew should have been carrying this coin, which they deemed idolatrous as well. Jesus shrewdly distanced himself from previous anti-government radicals and exposed hypocrisy during the same dialogue.

Compare how combative and shrewd Jesus is with how the ideal Christian man is expected to behave. The most active behavior Christian men are encouraged to partake in is fervent prayer about a situation. A Christian man is not supposed to call anyone a hypocrite or "brood of vipers" (Matthew 34:12) or "children of the devil" (1 John 3:10). Such confrontation would be considered worldly. This is irreverent language toward authority figures, which is part of the definition of profanity.

A Christian man isn't supposed to resist the events in his life. All events come from the hand of God, who is trying to teach him a lesson (usually humility). Too bad for us this lesson doesn't include learning how to become more shrewd and cunning—just like Jesus as seen in this exchange.

GOOD GUY REBELLION ROLL CALL

I'm forty-one and I have four sons. I've used parts of No More Christian Nice Guy *for devotions and father-to-sons gabfests. There have been times when I was a CNG and changed after I got tired of being people's footstool or seeing things go on that were plain wrong. And there are times I've pushed a belief or principle to the limits and upset and annoyed people (at work, at church), but would get phone calls or comments in person commending me for stepping up to the plate.*

I work with too many "nice guys." As I tell my sons, if you believe in something, stand up for yourself and defend it. Don't listen to the nay-sayers and doubters. If you don't stand up for something, you'll fall for anything. I'm getting this book for each of my sons!

—Derek

HOW BEING "NICE" RUINS LOVE AND MARRIAGE

What is life when wanting love?
Night without a morning.
—Robert Burns

How she said it was funny. *What* she said was awful and shows why this lesson, based on chapter 6, which touches a raw nerve in men, is so important for men in general and Christian men in particular.

"My single Christian girl friends and I have a saying," said this woman who works for a Christian publisher. "The ideal man to date has only been in the church for two years. That way he still has some masculinity left."

I wanted to argue, but dejection overcame me. My head dropped, and I nodded yes. Popular and trendy Christianity extracts masculinity, making CNGs unattractive to women—married or not. This is bad news for both married and single CNGs who want to be married.

Pretending to be "nice" all the time—being dishonest with your wants and needs, keeping under the radar of life with small living, fearing and discrediting your emotions, and constantly seeking the approval of others—is a recipe for disaster. It leads to problems across the board, none more painful than love and marriage. Statistically, for nice guys who break the odds and do find a wife, they are headed for divorce court. According to a groundbreaking study coauthored by Brad Wilcox of the University of Virginia, the "most important determinant of women's marital happiness is the emotional engagement of her husband." This is horrible news for CNGs because they are emotionally challenged in life. They are unable to provide the most wanted quality in a husband in America today.

VIVACIOUS WOMEN

It's not uncommon for passive men to marry outgoing women. You could say that our people marry their people. Opposites do attract—for a while, until they attack. The same qualities that attract people may well become the same qualities that push people apart. The top of every marriage certificate should read, "Marriage is about building bridges back to one another." This lesson will help you build a bridge of integrity back to your wife. It should also increase your chances of getting married, if that is your desire.

Think about the qualities that attracted you to your wife, ex-wife, or girlfriend. Make a quick list. Chances are, some of those qualities that you initially found attractive have also frustrated you. This is normal. Now think about the qualities that attracted your wife, ex-wife, or girlfriend to you. Did she complain about these qualities later? If so, what, if anything, did you do about it?

As I explained in this chapter, I figured that my marriage would eventually be toast if I didn't try something different. I had also heard that rigidity was the main cause of divorce, and this made sense to me, especially as I analyzed the marriages of my friends that ended in divorce. So I purposed in my mind to try something different. Exactly what it was, I didn't know, but I was willing to try. My wife joined me.

Jot down the complaints your wife, ex-wife, girlfriend has/had about you. Do you think they are true? (Note: Avoid judging yourself too harshly about this. Just be factual for now. Just because these problems hold you down now doesn't mean it will always be this way. Like a lost hiker, you need to know where you are so you can figure out where you need to be. There's no shame in admitting this.)

If a complaint is true, write down the word that represents its opposite. For example, if she complained that you're passive, write down assertive. If she said you were fearful, write down bold—and while you're at it, write down loving, because love trumps fear every time.

SECRET CONTRACTS

Beginning on page ninety, I list some of the marriage woes that I helped create in my own marriage thanks to the CNG problem.

One of the quickest ways passive men get in trouble with wives is by being dishonest with their sexual wants and needs. Some men even think it's not right to have normal wants and needs. They find themselves in a dilemma: they want something, but they don't feel they can be honest about it. So they create a secret agreement with their wives, an agreement their wives never agreed to. They never had a chance.

This secret contract goes like this: I'll show you affection, then you show me more affection later.

But their wives are in the dark. Some turn to the women-substitute called pornography.

Think about the times you have either been angry or pouted about your lack of sex. Did you make your want clear to your wife, or were you like most CNGs and felt uncomfortable being honest?

How can you be more honest with your wants and needs in the future?

SACRIFICING TOO MUCH

Many Christian men have been told to sacrifice their entire being for their wives. This, they are told, makes them Christlike. Many have been told to expect nothing in return for their sacrifices and to require little, if anything, from their wives. If women were told to expect little, if anything, from their marriage, what would such a message (and messenger) be called?

Think about the effective leaders you know or have been exposed to in books and other media. Do they require little or nothing from those they lead?

Why have men been told this?

What does this message tell us about how parts of the church approach a man's normal wants and desires?

In what ways can we correct this message so we can create *genuine* domestic harmony instead?

The distinction between virtuous sacrifice and *sacrificing who you are* goes deeper than many people realize. People who go through life requiring little from their relationships also don't possess much power and energy, and they don't garner much respect. They specialize in low-voltage living, which makes them unattractive.

Observe people who possess low-voltage lives. How do they present themselves to others? How do other people respond to them? When in leadership, how do others respond?

What are the names that we give people who possess no unique interests and independent life? Think about these names in the context of marriage. What tone does it create?

WHAT'S HOLDING YOU BACK?

As chapter 5 explains, many CNGs are headed for divorce court since more wives than husbands file for divorce. And contrary to our common perception that women divorce men due to abuse (around 6 percent) and infidelity (some studies show that for every five unfaithful husbands, there are four unfaithful wives), the reason they file has more to do with "not feeling loved or appreciated" than any other reason.

CNGs don't do love well because fear acts like plastic wrap around their hearts. They don't receive love well and they don't give it well either. Many are a divorce statistic waiting to happen.

Fear of being thought of as weak and rejected is a large reason why guys just won't open up to their wives or girlfriends. They know our weaknesses better than anyone else. We know that no one other than our wives (for some men it's still their mother) can plunge a dagger deeper into our already fearful emotional life.

So we need to open up—but we must be wise about how we do it. Part of being wise as a serpent is protecting your heart from unnecessary suffering. So you need to answer this fundamental question: Is your wife or girlfriend a woman of basic goodwill? By basic goodwill, I mean an imperfect person, a sinner who makes mistakes, who may get angry with you from time to time, and at moments can even be petty (like you), but when you think about her overall behavior, you conclude that she's in your corner. She really wants you to do well. She proves this with her words and deeds. She provides good though not perfect advice, help, support. She cannot be characterized as someone who belittles, shames, or demeans who you are.

My experience with the women of CNGs is that most still possess a basic goodwill. They genuinely care for their guy and they want to do their part. They are willing to change, if that's what it takes (usually they aren't the problem). These women are strong and I admire them. I sometimes give them high fives. My wife and I even wrote a book for such women to help them better understand their CNG and what they should and shouldn't do to help him. The book is called *Married But Not*

Engaged: Why Men Check Out and What You Can Do to Create the Intimacy You Desire.

But I have to warn that there are a minority of women who aren't of goodwill. Perhaps they possessed goodwill when they got married, but their CNG helped it die with a death by a thousand passive stabbings. If so, then the death of their goodwill is tragic but understandable.

Then there are women who never possessed basic goodwill. They are dangerous and disturbed. Man Eaters. I hear from them, but it's rarer still. They don't like me, but I consider their disdain a compliment, since the weight of a person can be measured by the caliber of his enemies. Jesus said to pray for your enemies; he ever said you couldn't have any. These women gun for me because they like their men weak and pliable. I'm the right kind of dangerous to them.

If the gal in your life is not a woman of basic goodwill toward you (you likely played a role in the destruction of this goodwill with your frustrating Nice Guy behavior), then sharing your heart is not wise. Goodwill has to be rebuilt, and we write about how to do this in *Married But Not Engaged*. It would be best to see a counselor.

If she possesses goodwill, consider yourself blessed. Then consider the following:

Chances are, she shares her inner world with you. And chances are that you don't take this as an opportunity to attack her. Why do you think she'll somehow hurt you?

Where do you think this troubling reaction came from?

Think about the moments when you wanted to be more intimate but weren't.

What held you back?

If you could be assured that no harm would come to you, what would you say and do?

Now think about that harm you feared.

Give it a name. Analyze it.

Is it real? (Good Guy hint: If you have a hard time saying what you really feel, write it down and let the words stew for a while until you flesh out what you're really trying to say. Take your time.)

BETTER UNDERSTANDING OF COMMITMENT

When we talk about commitment, what we often think about is *endurance*—as enduring marriage when we don't feel like it. Though sticking in there through thick and thin is a part of most every marriage, this is not an accurate understanding of this misused word. A better understanding is extremely helpful to a CNG to create a happier marriage. Here's why:

Commitment, as it relates to marriage, is best understood as applying yourself to a task or goal. The virtue of commitment is no passive pursuit. It doesn't mean to just hang in there without complaining. CNGs are all too good at just hanging in there because it's often a passive act. It's not a virtue when a person is too afraid to exercise enough courage to try something new. In regard to marriage, sometimes just hanging in there is no different than a boat that has lost its motor on the high seas. It's a passive presence prone to flounder before it capsizes.

Commitment is a rugged, positive, down-to-business act. It seeks out problems before they happen. It anticipates, scans, confronts. It's the look in the eye of a forward-looking man. It's the broad shoulders of protection and vulnerability. It's a chest plate willing to take bullets—and feel pain from those bullets.

GOOD GUY WORKOUT

In what ways can you show commitment to your marriage today? What area comes to mind that your gut tells you needs to be addressed? Now go be proactive without getting angry. Address the problem and don't condemn the person behind the problem. Remember, the goal of the Good Guy Rebellion is to create a healthier situation for everyone—not to get back at people. Revenge makes small people smaller.

BONUS INFORMATION FOR SINGLE CNGS

Among the most painful correspondence I receive are from single CNGs. They often behave in ways that ensure they will remain single, and many don't see it. It should be apparent by now why: they have a small view of themselves and they follow a misguided church message that makes them unattractive to women. This section helps you single CNGs see where you're going wrong and what to do to increase your chances at lasting love.

Women consistently rank confidence and a sense of humor as the top characteristics that they find attractive in men. And fear, which owns the heart of every CNG, is the sworn enemy of confidence.

We all know the Scripture: Perfect love casts out fear. Well, the opposite is also true: fear casts out love. So the place to begin, single CNG, is to get a handle on what fear is doing to your life. We'll deal more with that in Lesson 11.

Gut Time: In what ways has your CNG problem ruined your dating life? Be specific.

GOOD GUY WORKOUT FOR SINGLE CNGS

To put it bluntly, single CNGs who want to be married need to grow a life, increase their exposure to single women, and employ strategy. Ask yourself, *How can I incorporate these changes into my life soon?*

- Express self-confidence, which you aid by pursuing interests that you are good at.
- Show excitement with life, which you aid by figuring out which settings make you feel happiest and most alive.

- Cultivate opinions and an independent spirit. While on a date, disagree with her without being obnoxious and without shrinking back. Your independent spirit may also include disagreeing with your minister on a non-essential of the faith. This doesn't make you a sinner. It helps you become a better thinker. It may mean refusing to sing words to worship songs that you think aren't true but feel pressure to sing anyway. Singing words you don't believe is being dishonest.

- Get active. Start an exercise problem or change your existing one to be around women more.

- Talk to women—older, younger, attractive, less attractive, taller, shorter, you get the picture. The goal is to become more comfortable around them and enjoy them for who they are. Women possess a unique, mystifying quality. Revel in it.

- Resist trying to control everything that happens while on dates. Romance is the mingling of wills and desires that is allowed to become a new creation. Trying to control this creation often kills it. Not trying to control everything takes the pressure off, helping you become you.

- Feed optimism in your life by listening to hopeful music and reading uplifting books. (Guys tend to like nonfiction, so read a biography about someone you admire. It may encourage you to be more like that person.)

- Don't gush on and on too early about your romantic wants and desires. You aren't required to tell her everything you think. Be shrewd.

- Don't appear needy while on dates and don't tell her she's beautiful on the first date either. Many women find this creepy.

- Calling the day after a date is tricky business. For some women it's seen as being needy. Give it a few days. If the date went well, she won't forget you. Strategizing to win a woman's affection is not a sin. It's a compliment.

- Set goals and take realistic steps to achieve them. This will help you appear forward-moving and dynamic.

- Figure out the area of your life where it's easiest to be assertive, and do something assertive this week. Undertake a challenge that builds your character and is meaningful in other ways, such as helping others.

- Eat better and get enough rest.

- Pursue a hobby that helps you feel alive and brings you into contact with single women.

- Consider taking up a musical instrument. It's an attractive and creative outlet.

- Smile, even when you don't feel like it. Don't fall into what I call fear face—suspicious eyes, hunched body posture. When fearful, breathe deep from your belly and relax your muscles, especially your shoulders.

- There's an old expression: Men fall in love through their eyes, women through their ears. Keep this in mind. Ask her questions about herself and really listen. Make eye contact when you do. (For more on this, pick up a copy of *Creative Conversation Starters for Couples* by Robert and Pamela Crosby. It lists thoughtful questions to ask while getting to know someone better. I still use them while on date nights with my wife. Among my favorite questions: Who made you feel important as a kid? Don't ask this unless you really want to know her and you are willing to handle her soul with care.)

- Don't worry about what's going to happen weeks or months from now. Just enjoy her company and potential friendship. This takes the pressure off.

- Don't forget to use your sense of humor. You might memorize a few funny lines.

- Gently tease her—but not about something sensitive, like her appearance. Here's an example from my dating life with my wife. One night after dinner I suggested we go for walk. Within a few steps I realized that Sandy meant business. She took off. Her pace was beginning to wind me, since she was a runner and I wasn't. After about five minutes of this unwelcome workout, I grabbed her by the shoulders and said, "Where's the finish line?" (I wasn't always a CNG.) She looked at me like, *Who are you, pal?* But then her expression and countenance changed. She liked how I spoke my mind and didn't let her run away with the show. I took charge with a light joke, and she found it very attractive. The right kind of teasing and joking shows a certain independence, that you aren't needy for her complete approval. If she can't take appropriate teasing and joking, then she's got some soul work to do. (I don't trust people without a sense of humor.) If you can't take teasing, there's a problem too. You need to lighten up.

- Be less serious. Enjoy life more. Go out with your buddies more. Welcome, don't push away, their masculine energy.

- Listen to a new style of music. (Don't be confined to the idea that you have to listen to "Christian music." I hate to say it, but much Christian music isn't musical.)

- Go see a genre of movie you normally don't see.

- Consider getting a dog if you don't have one. They are great conversation starters and cause you to be more active than you might be otherwise. I recommend terriers. Their bold personas are a case study in attitude and personality.

Bestselling men's author Steve Arterburn said, "Confidence comes with acceptance of your self and the direction you are going based on the decisions you make. Healthy women love confident men because they have a strong team member vs. one that has to be nursed or fixed."

SILVER LINING

Single CNGs can be grateful for one thing: they did not get married while living the CNG deceptive lifestyle. They avoided a lot of pain, sin, confusion, and heartache. And they also avoided marrying the dangerous or foolish kind of women attracted to such men who in turn are often addicted in some degree to pornography.

WHAT A WOMAN'S LOVE DID TO (THEN SINGLE) PHILIP YANCEY

Then I fell in love. Janet and I drew together for all the wrong reasons—mainly we sat around and complained about the oppressive atmosphere of the [Christian] school—but eventually the most powerful force in the universe, love, won out. I had found someone who pointed out everything right with me, not everything wrong. Hope aroused. I wanted to conquer worlds and lay them at her feet. For her birthday I learned Beethoven's *Sonata Pathétique* and asked, trembling, if she would be the first audience to hear me play. It was an offering to new life, and to her who had called it forth."
(Philip Yancey, *Soul Survivor: How My Faith Survived the Church*)

GOOD GUY REBELLION ROLL CALL

When I would find a girl I thought was marriage material, I would become her best friend. I would also obsess over her and drive her crazy, usually telling her I love her way too soon. Or even if I met a girl that I liked, I would act all weird and different around her. I'd find myself saying stuff that just wasn't true. [Note: See how nice guys aren't honest?] I pretended to be interested in things that I normally didn't care about.

In my relationship with my fiancée, I would do things not out of love but out of conflict avoidance. . . . I was doing everything out of duty! I had many opportunities to end the relationship, but I did not. I developed a passive attitude—just drifted along and didn't work out problems. You helped me see that this approach wasn't cutting it. That it was hurting both me and my fiancée. You helped me talk

about the fact we weren't compatible (something we both knew).
During this break-up I kept repeating to myself what you said, "Be
good, not nice."
—Mike

ON BECOMING WISE/CUNNING/SHREWD AS SERPENTS

The Barna Research Group studied the character of individuals who assume positions of leadership in our churches. Barna studied their sense of calling from God to leadership, the nature of their character, the strength of their competencies, and the aptitude they possess for leadership.

Of the thirteen character traits studied, *wisdom ranked the lowest.*

No wonder being wise as a serpent isn't emphasized in our churches. We all suffer because of it, especially CNGs and those in their lives.

Wise as a Serpent 0. Innocent as Doves 1.

WE'RE MEN, NOT EUNUCHS

EROTICISM AND THE SONG OF SONGS

Life lost magic when it lost its eroticism. Eroticism, that elixir of passion, that thirsty desire to uncover the mystery of all life has to teach us, is noticeably absent from our being. . . . God wished to free us not only from the chains of slavery, but from the bane of an unanimated existence. God did not wish for us simply to exist, but to live; to subsist not merely with necessities, but with magic. For this reason He gave us the Song of Songs to teach us the power of discovering an erotic existence.

—Rabbi Shmuley Boteach

When surveyed, Christian women express higher levels of marital satisfaction than any other group, religious or not. But no such survey gives Christian men reason to celebrate domestic life. At the heart of their dissatisfaction is unmet sexual intimacy.

Like this man, who heard me talk about this problem and then revealed his deepest pain to me.

His conservative, modest, meek, humble, and by most standards, seemingly ideal Christian wife doesn't desire sex with him.

"I want her to wear more attractive clothing," he tells me. He wants to be attracted to her, not other women. It's his game plan to fight lust, he says, and it makes sense to me.

"Does she want to wear more attractive clothing?" I ask.

"She says it makes her feel uncomfortable," he says.

"How frequently do you have sex?" I ask.

"About once a month. Sex makes her *uncomfortable*," he says, not proud of his answer. His eyes look down.

"Does she enjoy it when you do?" I ask, hoping against all odds.

"Not really," he admits. "But she tells me it's okay with her if I masturbate," he says.

How thoughtful, I think to myself.

What an assault on his manhood. What complete disregard for his healthy, normal sexual desires. What bait and switch. If this man were to commit adultery, I hope Christians around them would have enough common sense and sympathy to say she played a part in his marital dissatisfaction. But I fear this is asking too much from portions of the church, which has unfairly told men that if there's a problem with their marriage, it's the guy's fault. We have been told that wives intrinsically respect good leadership. This is true of wives who possess basic goodwill toward their husbands, and not true for those who don't.

Common sense tells us that not everyone respects or follows great leaders. If so, then Jesus would never have been crucified, and Abraham Lincoln and Martin Luther King Jr. would not have been torn apart by assassins' bullets. The list of great leaders who were attacked goes on.

Yet this wounded man's affection remains constant for a woman who tells him to degrade himself, when the real answer includes her pushing past fear of intimacy to create marital harmony.

What names would a husband be called if he told his wife to masturbate in order to relieve normal sexual desires?

Are these names given to wives who commit the same behavior?

If not, discuss why.

WARNING: PROCEED WITH CAUTION

CNGs are good at blaming other people for their lack of happiness in life. At the top of their list is the lack of quantity and quality of their sexual relations. So do yourself a big fat favor, something that will save you and your wife a lot of grief: DON'T BLAME YOUR WIFE. DON'T GET ANGRY WITH HER. True, some wives may play a role in this. But this work you're doing right now of going deeper and getting better isn't about other people and trying to change their ways. It's about changing *your* ways to everyone's benefit.

Expressing anger (and sarcasm) in this delicate area will make intimacy even more elusive. Channel your energy instead into the following exercise. This is how you become wise as a serpent, Grasshopper.

And remember the difference between being bossy and being bold. Bossy people enjoy giving other people orders. This isn't leadership and it sure isn't being bold. Being bold includes a willingness to face uncertainty with a sense of confidence. When it comes to sexual intimacy, it also includes a willingness to be vulnerable.

BECOMING WISE AS SERPENTS

Couples with healthy sex lives often set time aside for sexual intimacy—especially if they have little ones around. But being so direct makes CNGs uncomfortable, even when such wise behavior helps them avoid sin.

Why does making a smart decision like this make you uncomfortable?

What proactive steps can you make today that will address this real problem in your life?

GOOD GUY REBELLION ROLL CALL

Here's a letter from a thoughtful reader, a wife, who brings up some fundamental issues that we guys need to consider:

> When I read chapter 6, I saw a lot of our early marriage—a lot of me in my past is in that chapter. There were two factors: One, I felt unprotected by my husband from my mother-in-law. And two, the hard work of real life, having babies and all, exhausted me. I didn't see this at the time, but I know it's true now.

Guys, what can you do today to help take the pressure off your wife so she can relax more and not be so tired?

What can you do to help your wife feel more protected?

GOOD GUY REBELLION ROLL CALL

> I was married for five years. I felt God put us both together, and I willingly gave up sex for months at a time because she wasn't in any way attracted to me. Paul, I have issues. I know this. I've had NO SPINE for years. My problem is this: the walking on me, taking me for granted, etc., gets to me, and I become a rotten sob. I have a relationship with the Jesus you talk about: the sugar puff type. All nice, no conflict. I want to get this out of me. I've always been the nice guy who finished last. Why? Because women like strong, confident men, not wusses. I just need some kind of game plan as to how to change without being a butthead.
>
> God bless you for putting this out there—I NEED it!
>
> —John

John's nice-to-nasty behavior is a standard operating procedure for CNGs. Does John's behavior ring a bell? What advice would you give John so that his legitimate sexual desires would have been met, helping him avoid resentment and related sins? Chances are, it's the same changes you need to follow.

FRUMP SYNDROME

The Frump Syndrome, as Dr. Laura calls it, is what happens to many women after marriage—and definitely after having children. "Symptoms of which include wearing flannel pajamas and socks, or sweatpants with oversized T-shirts, to bed instead of some girly thing with lace; not shaving legs or grooming nails; not washing, styling or even combing hair. . . ."

What attracts men to women, she writes, is their femininity, "and femininity isn't only about appearance, it's also about behaviors. Looking womanly and behaving sweetly and flirtatiously are gifts wives give to their husbands. This gift communicates that the husband is seen as a man, not just a fix-it guy, the bread-winner, or the sperm donor."

But the Frump Syndrome is a two-way street, guys! It's more than just looks too. It also includes unattractive thinking and moods that haunt CNGs. Here's a checklist of common guy mistakes that impede intimacy. Eradicate them from your life:

Going to the bathroom with the door open
Not brushing your teeth regularly
Paying more attention to hobbies and television than her and your children
Smelly body parts
An air of anger or that you're somehow a victim
Putting her down, often with sarcasm

Putting other people down

Pouting

Excessive complaining

Selfish sexual behavior

Being a slob

Somberness

Inability to make important decisions

BALANCING ROMANCE

Romancing a spouse is supposed to be a two-way street, but I'm wracking my brain trying to think of one movie, book, play, or conversation on the radio, when I've heard a man describe his wife as romantic. I can't think of one time. Is it that men don't need romancing? No, don't believe that. Is it that men define romancing differently? Probably. Is it that men don't get much romancing? Definitely.

—Dr. Laura, *Proper Care & Feeding of Husbands*

What are ways that your wife likes to be romanced? Read to her your answers and see if they're accurate. Modify your list as you need and keep it handy.

How do you define romance? What are ways that you would like to receive romance? (Note: This is not a "girly" question. It's a way to fortify your bridge of intimacy, monogamy, and marital harmony. These are masculine goals too. And remember, the Good Guy Rebellion is about kicking out the walls of our Man Box and becoming more sensitive in areas, not less. We redefine suffocating terms for the benefit of all.)

Share this information with your wife in a relaxed setting.

A DEEPER UNDERSTANDING OF INTIMACY

Numerous wives of CNGs say that chapter 6 helped them understand their husband's normal sexual desires with greater discernment, which has more to do with accurate perceptions than values, a common misunderstanding we hear in church.

Take time to read this chapter together. Don't be in a rush, and don't use it as an opportunity to show your wife where she has gone wrong. The goal is to reach a better understanding of this important issue. There are some funny parts in this chapter. Laugh together! Discuss whatever thoughts come to mind, making sure that you don't condemn each other.

The physical pleasure of intimacy doesn't need much explaining to us guys. But what needs to be pointed out is that guys desire sex in order to feel emotional closeness with their wives. So it would be helpful for wives to think of their husband's sexual desire this way: Instead of thinking that he just wants sex, what many men are really after is feeling close to you.

In order to create better sexual quality, what are ways that you can communicate to your wife that what you really want from her is emotional intimacy?

GOOD GUY WORKOUT

The next time you're feeling in the mood, ask yourself: Am I hungry for physical pleasure or emotional intimacy? If you've been married for a while, you should know the difference.

Sometimes sex is like fast food: it doesn't set any records for quality, and you don't linger over it. It's the reproductive, physically pleasurable kind, and that's great. It should also be like a fine meal, a lingering time of immense intimacy, or you're flirting with disaster (remember that statistic on divorce explained earlier?).

During the times when you desire emotional intimacy, and you find that your spouse does not, consider abstaining until the situation changes. This is important because CNGs often settle for unfulfilling sex. The only way that this is going to change is if you do something about it. Going down the same wrong path, getting the same wrong result, makes matters worse for everyone. You are left feeling empty and resentful.

Explain why you are abstaining, how you want greater emotional connection and you're willing to wait for it. A normal, healthy woman should be flattered by your desire to be closer to her. This is an exercise in genuine leadership. Give yourself a medal.

THE RISK OF INTIMACY

David Schnarch writes in an article entitled "Joy With Your Underwear Down": "What is most human about human sexuality is our unique capacity for intimacy. It takes guts as well as gusto to get any of the glory. . . . [S]ex that comes naturally is reproductive sex. Intimate sex, however, is a learned ability and an acquired taste."

If intimacy is an acquired taste, how specifically do you acquire it? Does this include taking risks, being vulnerable?

Since we aren't born with this knowledge, where would a wise man look?

What can you do today to bolster intimacy, a confidence-building behavior that also decreases your chances of separation and divorce?

Schnarch continues, "Sex can be more than just a euphemism for 'making love.' It can be the actual process of increasing love, of sharing it, of whetting our appetite for it, and of celebrating life on its own terms. This process . . . is actually built into the nature of committed relationships. It happens almost spontaneously; the hard part is going through it. . . . Intimacy . . . is not always soothing and doesn't always 'feel good.' It is, however, how we forge ourselves into the people we would like to be."

When is intimacy not soothing?

What have you learned during these moments?

In what ways have you become a better person? If you haven't, what can you do to change this situation?

THE BLESSINGS OF BEING HUMAN

Strange things happen when we have sex at the limits of our potential. That we hear so little about the spiritual side of sex reflects how few people ever reach their sexual potential.

There is time stoppage. It is a consequence of profound involvement.

There's also a lack of awareness of pain. I work with people who have arthritis. I advise them to have sex in the morning, so they will have less pain—but to have less pain they have to be involved.

There is a laserlike focusing of consciousness. There is often a vacation-like sense of transportation.

Age shifting is another phenomenon. You may be holding your partner's face in your hands and suddenly see, in a very loving way, what he or she will look like older, or exactly what [she] looked like when [she] was eight years old. It is very moving. (David Schnarch, "Joy With Your Underwear Down.")

Are these experiences foreign to you?

Does this good gift from God frighten you, especially the aspect of losing control?

What might you gain by losing control, by letting sexual energy unfold as it will, on its own terms?

Do you label this as sinful? If so, why?

Discuss these attributes of greater intimacy with your spouse, these blessings of being human. Observe her reactions. If they make her uncomfortable, find out why.

GOOD GUY REBELLION ROLL CALL

Sexuality is not natural. This is the most damaging lie. Basically, my parents and the church harped on us so much about not having sex, that it equated into not dating girls or being comfortable around them for years, when I came to believe that "everything could potentially lead to sex.'' It blurred the lines between God-given desires and lust.

—Aaron said this is one of the three biggest lies he learned from his Christian home and church.

Many CNGs feel ashamed to be sexual. Think about your view of sex that you got from church. How would you describe it?

For example, was sex portrayed as good and healthy, but something to be restricted only in marriage?

Was it portrayed in a dirty way?

How did your experience shape what you think about sex now?

CONFUSED TO VILIFIED: OUR CULTURE'S VIEW OF MASCULINITY

Testosterone. It's deadlier than the a-bomb. More insidious than pollution. . . . Whenever possible, I work with women.
—Popular blogger Jesse Kornbluth, Swami Uptown, for *Beliefnet.com*

Ralph Ellison wrote the American classic *The Invisible Man* to protest prejudice against African Americans. A similar prejudice exists against men in general. I call it genderism, and no great novel has yet to be written to change this life-draining problem.

GROWING UP WITHOUT DADS

Many readers of CNG write about what it was like growing up without a dad. For many it felt weird and isolating, as if somehow they were kept at an arm's length from a part of themselves that they weren't able to name. This letter from a thirty-something man who I'll call Steve, is just one of many I've received about this problem. Note his anger and resentment for being told to live by feminine sensibilities:

GOOD GUY REBELLION ROLL CALL

My parents divorced when I was twelve, and I was raised by my mom. "Everyone says you're such a nice boy," is what my mom would tell me. So I learned early on that that is what people wanted, or so I thought. Looking back, however, I can see how people were drawn to men who were strong and free to share opinions and take a stand.

People would talk to me as a child out of an obligation because I was "such a nice boy." I even had one older person tell me she hoped her granddaughter would find someone as nice as me to marry. I now want to puke big chunks.

Now I can see what being raised by such a woman has caused. My wife has no respect for me and is frustrated that I have had no passion, direction, dreams, or desires. We never argue and our peers even say, "You guys are perfect." I gorged myself on being nice.

When my wife and I struggled with intimacy in our marriage, I thought I was being chivalrous by not pressing the issue or talking about it. I thought my needs and wants were not important and buried them below a manhole of heavy resentment. I went into marriage with the goal of playing preventive defense—to not get divorced—instead of being passionate, adventurous, dreaming, and taking risks.

In football they say playing preventive defense prevents you from winning. Playing preventive defense in marriage is equal to allowing anything to take place as long as it is in front of you and you feel as though you are in control. You never blitz or fight back because that would not be nice. Every chunk of yardage that is given up puts you closer to the red zone and eventually leads to a devastating score that paralyzes you flat on your back.

—Steve

Steve's experience is not every guy's experience who grew up without a father. But it is for many.

For those who grew up with a mother but not a father:

What understanding of being male did you receive? It helps to write down any word or phrase that comes to mind. This process can be slow at first, but then your memories and thoughts will flow more easily. It's not uncommon to have a hard time keeping up with your thoughts once your ideas flow.

Think of the boys you knew who had dads at home. How did they behave? For example, did they appear more secure while in the limelight or while in difficult situations? Did you admire them, resent them, hate them? If yes, why?

Women tend to extract masculinity from their boys in two ways: ignorance and hence a mishandling of masculinity; or a disdain for masculine energy and behavior, so they hunt it down, making sure their sons remain weak and pliable. Most CNGs fall into the first camp, a minority the latter.

Which do you fall into?

If in the first camp, how specifically was your masculinity mishandled?

In what ways does it affect you today?

Are you or your wife passing this view on to your sons?

In what ways may you have to rescue your son(s) from having his budding masculinity destroyed?

If you grew up in a home that featured a disdain of masculinity, realize that more damage was done to you. This isn't the end of the world. There's hope. I was also in the second camp. It just means the problem and lies went deeper into you. Still, you are never without hope.

Think of the moments when your masculinity was hunted down. Think of it in terms of homicide.

When did it happen?

Describe the crime scene.

What instruments were used? (Hint: the weapon is usually not physical but mental or emotional. A lie is often the handle that fits them all.)

Were there witnesses? Have you ever talked with them? Know that some witnesses are trustworthy, some aren't. Use your instincts on this one. And don't make their testimony fit into a "Christian" mold. Remember, all truth is God's truth.

Now, most importantly: what was the motive of your attacker? (In most cases, it wasn't about you. The problem wasn't you. It wasn't your fault.) Before you answer this question, keep reading.

Motives are a tough arena of life. You may be tempted to assume that the person who did this and other bad things to you was motivated by evil. That the person herself was evil. I want to caution you against this thinking. Though I believe in evil, that we receive aid in doing evil things, and that some people may indeed embody evil, such people are rare. (I had a long conversation with the late Dr. Scott Peck on this topic, who issued a similar warning.)

Something more common and human took place. Most likely, something painful was done to her, probably by a man. She associates pain with masculinity, so she fought to keep that pain out of her life. She was attacking males in general when she saw this maleness in you. It's understandable, but it's also destructive.

I'm writing this to help you frame this issue from another perspective, not to dismiss it and say it was okay. It wasn't. My hope is that you see the fallout clearly, that you take steps today to fix this problem you face, and you have greater understanding about the person who did the damage. If you don't, you will likely fall into rage, resentment, and hatred. All will diminish you and stop you from becoming a Christian Good Guy.

Now answer that question above.

For men who did grow up with a father:

What are some practical ways that you can help men you know who didn't grow up with a dad? How can you help fatherless boys today?

What did your father do to weaken your confidence in being a man? In what ways did he give you strength and confidence?

> *We're a generation raised by women. We're the middle children of history, man. No purpose or place. We have no Great War no Great Depression. Our Great War's a spiritual war. Our Great Depression is our lives.*
>
> —Tyler Durden (Brad Pitt) in *Fight Club*

BALL OF CONFUSION: DEFINITIONS OF MAS-CU-LIN-I-TY

1905: Having the qualities of a man; virile, not feminine or effeminate; strong; robust. (Note: the word "effeminate" used to be synonymous with "nice.")

2005: The state of being a man or boy; those qualities conventionally supposed to make a man a typical or excellent specimen of manhood, traditionally physical strength and courage. (Note the qualifying words "conventionally," "supposed," and "traditionally." Our dictionary can't be brought to take a stand on this word and the issues it represents.)

ADJUSTING OUR CULTURAL FREQUENCY: WE'RE DISPOSABLE—AND A LITTLE BRAIN-DEAD

A study that compared gender stereotypes common in the 1970s to those held in the 1990s found that while female stereotypes have improved, those of their male counterparts have soured. Women are characterized as "intelligent, logical, independent, adventurous, dependable," and "skilled at relationships." Men? In the 1970s they were thought of as "assertive" and "savvy." But in the 1990s: "jealous, moody, fussy, temperamental, deceptive, narrow-minded," and "heedless of consequences." The report characterized this view of men as "negative masculinity." Like I wrote, shame for being male is practically in our DNA.

A female talk-show host on TBN (Trinity Broadcast Network) referred to all men as "brain-dead." What would happen if a male talk-show host said that all women were "brain-dead"?

For decades men have been called sperm donors. What would happen if men called women "egg donors" or merely "breeders"?

Do you feel weird or uncomfortable disagreeing with a woman, even if she's obnoxious, wrong, or even dangerous? If so, where does this discomfort come from?

In what other ways has our culture's view of masculinity affected you?

BOYS ARE DISPOSABLE TOO

This chapter reports the popularity of a line of clothing that degenerates boys. Slogans on this line of clothing read:

> Boys are Stupid. Throw Rocks at Them.
> Boys are Smelly—Throw Garbage Cans at Them.
> The Stupid Factory—Where Boys Are Made.

It's time for a culture check. Replace the word "Boy" in the above slogans with the word "Girls." Then replace it with "Cats."

Chances are, you would find yourself the epicenter of protest and media attacks.

But why hasn't the media done the same for boys?

What does this tell us about our culture?

SOME STARTLING STATISTICS

Though men have been told that their nature is dangerous and "heedless of consequences," statistics tell a different story.

- Two-thirds or more of all divorces involving couples with children are initiated by mothers, not fathers.
- According to the U.S. Department of Justice, nearly two-thirds of confirmed cases of child abuse and of parental murders of children are committed by mothers, not fathers. A 1999 report by the U.S. Department of Health and Human Services revealed that, adjusting for the greater number of single mothers, a child is five times more likely to be murdered by a single mother than by a single father.
- The same study reveals that children are 88 percent more likely to be seriously injured from abuse or neglect by their mothers than by their fathers.
- For three decades, independent studies, including the study released in 2004 by the University of Michigan Institute for Social Research, have shown that men do their share of household labor.

Chances are, you have never heard these statistics before, other than in *No More Christian Nice Guy*. This is not due to a media conspiracy. It is due to a cultural prejudice against men in general. You may not be able to control what comes out of your television set or what's printed in your local newspaper, but you have a lot of control over what comes out of your mouth.

Think of ways that our culture's prejudice against men and masculinity has gotten into your thinking. Write down or discuss with your friends what are the common stereotypes about guys. Then think about ways that you can combat these stereotypes. One way is to take the stereotype (such as men are irresponsible) and apply it toward women. It helps you and others to see how ridiculous such stereotypes really are.

GOOD GUY WORKOUT
Masculinity and Sensitivity

Somewhere along the line, the Man Box got mighty small in one fundamental direction: It cut out sensitivity. This is the result of two profound forces: boys have been told not to express painful emotions; and guys, on average, are more than happy to avoid deep emotions because, improperly handled, they take a toll on guys. They often stir fearful and shameful feelings. We feel out of control.

In this chapter I talk about my own fear of deep emotion, made worse by the only time I saw my father cry. He appeared tormented. I wrote that I called this moment the Day of the Mighty Scissors. Most every CNG has one.

If possible, before doing the following workout, take a look at some pictures of your father (or father figure) when you were a kid. It helps to see him as he was back then, not as he is now. We all change.

Think of the time(s) when you saw your father cry. (If never, what does this tell you about him?)

Did his tears make you think that crying was a good thing? Did they frighten you?

What did your experience tell you about life? About how guys are expected to live?

When your children cry, especially your boys, do you recoil and try to dry the tears as soon as possible, or do you enter into his pain, being careful not to short-circuit it or belittle it?

Why, as Christian men, do we think boys and men shouldn't cry when Jesus did?

MISTER ROGERS: CHRISTIAN GOOD GUY

Some men were surprised by my defense of the late Mister Rogers in this chapter. But when you put my defense in the larger context of how the Good Guy Rebellion expands the Man Box to include more sensitivity and toughness, it makes sense. Mister Rogers also did me a lot of good as a kid, so I wanted to return the favor.

Elvis Costello has a great line of music that I want us to think about. He sang, "What's so funny about peace, love, and understanding?!" Blind traditionalism, as opposed to a genuine biblical understanding of life, causes some Christians to ridicule these life-giving attributes—and I just scratch my balding head. We need to stop this foolish thinking. Jesus cared a lot about peace, love, and understanding.

And so did Fred Rogers. His good work continues to lift children up across the globe. For some, he's the only gentle, kind, and virtuous person they regularly meet.

His tone was assuring, never condescending toward children. Now let's compare his tone to ours.

How would you describe your tone of voice and demeanor toward children?

Is there room for improvement? If so, how?

Mister Rogers consistently honed his message to children even after he achieved notoriety and fame. What can you do to bless the timid and the weak right now?

GOOD GUY REBELLION ROLL CALL

Great chapter. I realized some things about myself. It also caused me to think of more questions I need to answer. It caused me to wonder how you separate the spiritual from the physical. I want to have the big house and the family, but in some sense I feel like succeeding in life is sinful. Even when I was not into Christianity, I thought this way. I felt that I just needed to be passive and not go for anything in life because that would be wrong. I thought it was wrong to want anything in life because that puts God second.

—Tim

NICE GUY, NAÏVE GUY: HOW BEING NICE HURTS MEN AT WORK

Another arena where the "evan-jelly-cal" Christian Nice Guy problem becomes so maddening is in the workplace. This lesson, based on chapter 8, will help you gain a deeper understanding of what you need to do in order to make work *work* for a change.

GOOD GUY REBELLION ROLL CALL

I'm surrounded by "nice guys" at work, people who won't try anything new—even when it's pretty clear that the change will be good for the company. These guys all go to church, but when they see people more powerful doing things they know are wrong, they all look the other way like they don't see it. It drives me crazy.
—Robert

FUNDAMENTAL QUESTION

When surveyed, most say that they would not keep their current job if they didn't need the money. So for most people, they work to make an income. This fact is not a problem for successful people, but CNGs have a problem with it.

A lot of books for Christian men forget this fact, and instead emphasize the importance of sharing God's redemptive plan with co-workers and to bring God glory through work well done. These may be by-products of paid employment, but not the main reason we punch the clock throughout our lives.

Think about the jobs you've had, and then ask yourself: Why do I work?

If the answer is to receive an income and this feels selfish to you, do you know why you think this is selfish as opposed to just having normal wants and needs?

BONUS INFORMATION: TUGGING ON GREEN FRUIT

If you really want to spend more time sharing God's good news with others, you will likely be more successful doing it in places where people are seeking God. Most people simply don't go to work as part of a spiritual pilgrimage. If you've been around long enough, you've seen Christians witness to non-Christians at work. The distance between evangelical zeal and non-Christian indifference can be painful to see. A lot of green fruit gets tugged in the workplace, which is instructive since Jesus didn't force his message on people.

And if you want to bring God glory, it is often better done without the strings of money attached, which come with jobs. You will be less encumbered by having fewer people to please. Without the attachment of money, people are simply freer to be bolder.

I'm not saying God's redemptive plan shouldn't be shared at work. I am saying that you don't need paid employment to do it.

TRAP OF "PERFECT" WORK

Each time Microsoft releases a new operating system, let's just say, it has issues. We hear about "bugs" that require "patches." And each year, that company and its head guy, Bill Gates, makes a killing. (I'm thinking that I'm just going to start sending Bill Gates my money directly. He's going to get it eventually.) My point is that the richest man in the world oversees products that aren't perfect. They are flawed, and it doesn't stop Microsoft. If they held up production of a good operating system with the hope that it would be perfect someday, no operating system would be released. Microsoft doesn't let naïve ideas about perfection stop them.

But it stops CNGs, who are often bright men with good intentions but who are held down by an unattainable goal of perfection. This makes their workplace mistakes even harder on them and their families.

At the core of this disease to please is the desire to escape all potential criticism.

To this we have to ask: Does Bill Gates get criticized? There are Web sites and books devoted to picking this guy apart. Does he keep moving ahead anyway? You know the answer to that one, and I hope you're seeing a trend: successful people don't adhere to naïve notions of perfection.

In what ways do you try to appear perfect at work?

Some CNGs go above and beyond what's asked of them in order to appear perfect. If this describes you, then consider this: Has your devotion to "perfect" work, which can be better than other people's work, brought you just compensation?

CNGs enter the workplace trying to please a host of people, some of whom are un-pleasable, such as their parents, dead or alive.

Who are you really trying to please by adhering to such an unattainable standard?

What has been the result?

FEELING GUILTY ABOUT BEING REAL

I sat next to a successful Christian woman at an important fund-raiser for an organization where I was a board member. She asked me what I did and I told her. She asked me if I was happy. I said not really, and I proceeded to tell her about my frustration. Then I said, "But my employer has my best interest at heart." I was still president of the CNGA (Christian Nice Guy Association) then. This successful and philanthropic business owner was clearly shaken. She composed herself and told me, "Your boss may be a good person, but he's more concerned about himself than you. No one has your best interest in mind other than you."

A minister friend of mine had a similar eye-opening conversation with a church consultant. They brought him in when staff was struggling to keep work and home in balance. He had blunt news for my friend. "Your congregation as a whole doesn't care about you and your family. Don't get me wrong. Some of them do, but churches are so full of needy people that they can't see you are a person with a life outside of church. Their needs blind them to the real you. Don't let them steal your family, because they will if given the opportunity."

Chances are, you've been told that taking care of yourself vocationally is worldly. Where did you get this information?

Think of the successful people you know. How do they view their vocation?

If the main purpose of paid employment is to make an income, then what is wrong with fulfilling the main purpose of paid employment?

Christian men have been told that they should submerge their needs and wants (including raises) at work in order to bolster their Christian witness. This plays well into their flawed internal belief that taking care of themselves is greedy. Their families sometimes go without and marital strife occurs. None of this is a good witness.

If you feel it's greedy to ask for a raise, find out why.

BURNOUT: THE RESULT OF PERFECT WORK

CNGs not only waste energy trying to achieve the unachievable, they wear themselves (and others) out in the process. Here's a checklist to help you discover if you're in burnout's downward spiral (courtesy of *www.teamworks-works.com*).

- [ ] More and more, I find that I can hardly wait for quitting time to come so that I can leave work.
- [ ] I feel like I'm not doing any good at work these days.
- [ ] I am more irritable than I used to be.
- [ ] I'm thinking more about changing jobs.
- [ ] Lately I've become more cynical and negative.
- [ ] I have more headaches (or backaches, or other physical symptoms) than usual.
- [ ] Often I feel hopeless, like "who cares?"
- [ ] I drink more now or take tranquilizers just to cope with everyday stress.
- [ ] My energy level is not what it used to be. I'm tired all the time.
- [ ] I feel a lot of pressure and responsibility at work these days.
- [ ] My memory is not as good as it used to be.
- [ ] I don't seem to concentrate or pay attention like I did in the past.
- [ ] I don't sleep as well.
- [ ] My appetite is decreased these days (or I can't seem to stop eating).
- [ ] I feel unfulfilled and disillusioned.
- [ ] I'm not as enthusiastic about work as I was a year or two ago.
- [ ] I feel like a failure at work. All the work I've done hasn't been worth it.
- [ ] I can't seem to make decisions as easily as I once did.
- [ ] I find I'm doing fewer things at work that I like or that I do well.
- [ ] I often tell myself, *Why bother? It doesn't really matter anyhow.*

☐ I don't feel adequately rewarded or noticed for all the work I've done.

☐ I feel helpless, as if I can't see any way out of my problems.

☐ People have told me I'm too idealistic about my job.

☐ I think my career has just about come to a dead end.

Count up your check marks. If you agree with a majority of those statements, then you may be feeling burnout and be in need of professional help or counseling or, at least, a change in lifestyle.

One of the best ways to fight burnout is learning to say no. Here are ways that will help you refuse requests upon your time and energy:

When possible, kindly let people know in advance that you will say "no," and thank them for considering you.

Say no simply and politely.

Give a reason or explanation only if you choose to do so. Sometimes reasons create more chaos and show insecurity with your decision.

Avoid starting with an apology.

Repeat your message firmly and kindly until the other person hears your refusal. Consistently state your message.

Pay attention to your nonverbal messages. When you are secure with your reasons, you won't get visibly upset.

DIFFICULT WORK SETTINGS

Christian Nice Guys often find themselves in tough workplaces. This is not an accident. Remember, CNGs are attracted to organizations that function like a troubled family. True, it's weird. But yeah, it's true.

Manipulative bosses sense your weakness in this area. They know you are susceptible to the want of people's approval. And if they can tie the additional string of money to you, all the better for them.

In order to combat this problem, you need to see the problem for what it is, and you need to know why you work in the first place to help you avoid this problem in the future. (That's why this lesson begins with the fundamental question: Why do you work? This helps you remove the high-sounding but inaccurate spiritual veneer that you have been told to associate with paid employment.)

Most people have had a combination of good bosses and people who should not run a business. Think about the places you have worked and describe the kinds of bosses you have had. Remember, the goal is to steer you toward a good boss, now and in the future, or becoming a good one yourself. And just because someone's a Christian does not automatically qualify them to lead. Good leadership makes them qualified. It's a learned trait.

How specifically did your boss manipulate you? (For example, did he or she use approval that went beyond the normal employee-employer relationship and work standards?)

CNGs complain how religion was used again them. If religion was involved, what can you do to ensure it doesn't happen again? (Hint: Usually the religious concept was taken out of context. Review the religious message you were given in light of what the Bible actually says about the topic. For example, some people will tell you that you should behave like a slave to your boss, though such a statement is not found in the Bible. This will help you avoid this kind of manipulation in the future.)

Another way to turn work around is to form a Personal Life Mission. More on that in Lesson 11.

GOOD GUY WORKOUT

A great way to reduce unnecessary manipulation and related frustration in the workplace is to figure out ways to make additional income, ideally with non-labor-based income (such as trading securities), or limited labor-based income (such as fixing up homes and selling them, what's called "flipping" property). This will give you more confidence by making you less dependent on one source of income. If done right, you will receive more financial freedom that will give you more options. You'll feel more relaxed and far less needy.

Take an inventory of your skills and abilities. It helps to ask, *What do my friends say I'm good at?* Then match these skills with a way of making additional income and study these ways thoroughly. Most people have limited capital to work with. Be wise as a serpent with it.

BONUS INFORMATION: OWNING THE QUESTIONS, BEING PROACTIVE

Asking the right questions, and more importantly, being the owner of the right questions, can be among your best friends in the workplace. This is extremely important for CNGs because they spend too much time counter-punching in the workplace against people who use their weaknesses against them. You must become proactive or you will remain stuck.

While saying the following responses, remember two fundamental guidelines: Do not get angry. Do not make it personal. Instead, reframe the situation whenever possible in light of how the other person's behavior hurts the organization. Otherwise you will likely get sucked into a personal battle where you often lose.

Problem: A co-worker unfairly accuses you of letting personal matters interfere with your job performance. The co-worker does this during a staff meeting, and has gotten away with it in the past, making him bold. But not today.

Response: *Are you aware of the injustice you caused in our staff meeting this morning?*

Response: *What evidence do you have that my personal matters are affecting work?* Avoid getting emotional.

Problem: Someone takes a position against you for changes you've made that will help the company in the future but brings about unwelcomed change right now.

Response: *What changes can be made to the idea that will gain your support?* This puts the onus on the unreasonable critic, especially if those above him or her have approved of the idea.

Response: *Why do I feel that your opposition goes beyond the idea itself?* Ask this if you have documentation of defiance.

Problem: You discover, through a reliable witness, that someone is stabbing you in the back, saying you aren't pulling your share of the workload. This accusation is not true, and you can prove it if you have to.

Response: *What evidence do you have that I'm not carrying my share?* Spring this question out of nowhere, when the backstabber wouldn't have a reason to anticipate it.

If the person denies it, for whatever reason, say, *That denial may be real for you, but it's not real for me. In any case, don't ever let it happen again. Do we have an understanding?* When you knowingly go along with such false accusations, you are knowingly helping to cover up sin.

Problem: Someone loses her temper with you. It's unjustified. This is common for CNGs because people know they can get away with it. You burn inside but fail to defend yourself directly. You backstab instead, which is wrong and self-defeating. Remember, don't get angry in return.

Response: *What will you do to ensure that we never have a repeat of what just happened?* This response makes you appear big and above the problem, yet still sticking the blame where it belongs.

Response: *Do you feel justified in speaking to me this way?* If the answer is no, and the problem is not chronic, accept it. The workplace can be a boiler cooker sometimes. But if the problem is chronic and the person still apologizes, take a similar approach as above. *That apology may be real for you, but after all the times this has happened, it is not real for me. What I need instead is to have this never happen again.*

Problem: Someone misrepresents you, using your name to gain support for a project or related matter that in fact you do not support. You get angry, which is understandable. But again, do not show this anger.

Response: *What are your plans for retracting the statement that you falsely attributed to me?* Note, don't use this statement unless you have evidence. Be prepared to take it up the line if you have to. If the person proposes a remedy, give him or her a chance to save face.

Problem: Someone is deceiving you and you can prove it. It's more than a mistake. You think this problem is intentional. Someone is trying to use your passive ways against you.

Response: *Do you realize that I have serious doubts about the truth of what I'm hearing, and that I'm convinced you're digging yourself into a deep hole?* You're letting this person know that you won't tolerate this dishonest behavior (this is being truthful), and you're willing to give this person a chance to come clean (this is being gracious). This is how strong, virtuous, and successful people behave.

Response: *If I take you at your word, will you have to come back later and make excuses for what you're now telling me?* This is another gracious way of defending yourself and giving the person a chance to correct his mistake now, avoiding even worse consequences in the future. This is a win-win if the other person is willing to be honest.

(Based on *What to Ask When You Don't Know What to Say* by Sam Deep and Lyle Sussman.)

MASCULINITY: THE JOURNEY FROM NICE GUY TO GOOD GUY (PART 1)

Years ago, manhood was an opportunity for achievement, and now it is a problem to be overcome.
—Garrison Keillor

This lesson explains how masculinity isn't received as the result of a magic prayer, watching certain movies, or other quick fixes. It includes living by certain principles and, more importantly, avoiding certain behaviors that keep us in our CNG Sunday best—amiable, pleasant, and ineffective. This lesson helps us grow new backbones and stiffen the one we currently possess.

I write about Snivels, my coward within. Most of the time he stays in the background. I beat him back with every proactive step I take. You have a Snivels as well.

Give him a name.

I write about the specific areas where he tries to hold me down at home, work, church, relationships. Now it's your turn.

How specifically does he try to direct your steps? (Clue: look for the lie, the half-truth).

How specifically does he succeed?

In what ways do you mistake life's difficulties with God's sovereignty saying no?

What would have happened if Jesus confused difficulty for his Father's will?

How specifically has this misconception held you back in the past?

What about right now?

DEFINING REAL MASCULINITY

Don't look in the timid dictionary for help defining masculinity. I offer my own definition on page 160. Go through this definition, considering the following attributes:

Redemptive creativity

Protection

Purpose

Love

Write down opportunities in your own life that come to mind when you consider these attributes.

What is standing in your way? How can you be wise as a serpent to overcome what's stopping you?

Your journey toward a stronger form of masculinity must include something to struggle against. This will include an internal struggle (a personal quest for purity, moving toward the innocence of doves, as Jesus said) and an external struggle (a quest for truth, moving toward the wisdom of serpents, as Jesus said).

What is your main internal struggle, the sinful behavior that hinders you?

What is your main external struggle, the sinful behavior we collectively refuse to acknowledge as a culture and which fuels the fire of righteous indignation, protest, and reformation in you?

These two answers are keys to your masculine regeneration, part of your personal quest. Keep them handy. Keep them fed.

THREE TYPES OF MEN

Take another look at the three types of men, beginning on page 160. CNGs fall on the passive end of this spectrum. Nothing like stating the obvious, huh?

List the names of men you know or have seen in movies or have read about in books, especially in the Bible or biographies:

Passive:

Assertive:

Aggressive:

Spend time with the assertive ones. If or when appropriate, tell the persons you admire how they handle themselves, and ask them if they will share their thinking with you. Chances are, they will open your ears and eyes with behavior that doesn't fit the Christian stereotype but does fit the behavior found in the life of Christ.

LIVING BOLDLY

Christian Nice Guys have a hard time living boldly. It goes against their internal voice that tells them that the best way to live is to live small.

Matters are made worse when he attends a church that characterizes bold living as "worldly" and "fleshly." This goes against what the Bible says: "The righteous are as bold as a lion" (Proverbs 28:1) As one blogger writes, a Christian man is "stuck between The Rock and a hard place. No wonder he is so confused."

They are also petrified to live a larger life because this might include a more noticeable level of sin. We by and large prefer timid sins because it helps us avoid criticism. But what we're not noticing is how our timid sins get us into a lot of trouble as well, and they make us less the man we want to be and less like our Savior.

So that's why in this section I quote Martin Luther, who said that if you're going to sin, then "sin boldly." They are as forgivable as timid sins, so why worry?

Here's why CNGs worry: they think they have to do life perfectly. No room for mistakes. It should be obvious by now that this is an impossible standard and an excuse to avoid the courageous quest for bold living.

Worse, it spreads ruin to those in your care. This isn't fair to you or them. Our lives are our responsibility and sometimes our burden to improve. When we try to live perfectly, we are letting other people's disapproval and fear of their rejection run our lives. As I've said before, it takes more courage to live well than it does to live poorly.

Where did you get the idea that life doesn't make room for mistakes?

Whose disapproval are you trying to fight off?

Is it warranted?

Is it working? If not, why?

GOOD GUY WORKOUT
Dispensing Vitamin No

Telling people "yes" when you mean "no" is among the most prevalent lies CNGs tell. Our integrity takes a beating, and self-loathing is just a matter of time.

Think about the people who you need to give Vitamin No. Your gut is talking to you right now. It's telling you the names of people who push you around without regard for your feelings or your life in general. Write their names down. Tell them no, and expect some to try to manipulate you. They may demand that you explain yourself. Don't. You don't owe manipulative people an explanation. Our Savior sure didn't. But if you do choose to respond, give a vague response, such as, "This (activity or related matter) doesn't fit my larger goals. I wish you well in the future." If pressed, say it again, and leave it at that. Be prepared to end the conversation if you have to, or change it to another matter.

Warning: This is not a license to skirt your fundamental responsibilities as a husband, father, or employee. It is an opportunity to get pieces of your life back. (CNGs are skilled at fragmenting themselves to the point that they are unable to move effectively in any one direction.)

BETTER UNDERSTANDING OF INTEGRITY

We are used to thinking that personal integrity is limited to high moral principles and standards. This has been a staple message in men's ministry for decades. But this is an incomplete understanding of this often talked about virtue, and it is especially troublesome to CNGs. A life that possesses personal integrity also has a state of being sound and undamaged, much like a bridge that possesses structural integrity. But we of course are not inanimate objects. We are not made out of steel, though our lives should resemble it.

A life characterized by personal integrity is not formed solely through personal morality and ethics. It is also formed by wise decisions that maintain sound structure. Integrity cannot form if you don't create appropriate boundaries that ward off damage. Like the people who maintain the Golden Gate Bridge, integrity is proactive and assertive, not passive and reactive. Lives would be lost if they were the latter, and so will your life when you don't grasp this important distinction.

See why Jesus said to be wise as serpents and innocent as doves? An abundant life is not gained through high morals alone.

BESTOWED MAN TO MAN

Masculinity is a learned condition, which should give those of us with hardships in our past a bounce in our step, those of us who feel that we were behind the door when masculinity was handed out. It's not something you are born with, but something you evolve into. Like the flu, you get it from those who are close to you.

Go back to that list of Christian Nice Guys and Christian Good Guys that you created earlier in Lesson 1. Figure out which of the Christian Good Guys you have an opportunity to know better. A guy who just feels real when you talk to him, a guy who doesn't give the world a fake smile but still retains hope in his heart, language, eyes.

Warning: There is no perfect mentor out there. Given enough time, you'll discover that he too is a sinner just like you. Expect this. Do your best not to be shocked. Don't let naïve ideas about perfection stop you from learning from him. Remember, there are not two groups of men: those who do everything perfect and have all the answers and the rest of us who don't.

P-R-O-A-C-T-I-V-E

Being proactive is a main ingredient in the chemotherapy that fights your CNG cancer. I can't state this enough. You must become proactive or you're not going to make it. You have to move and exert your will.

Think about the energy you put into defending yourself from both real accusations and ones you think are coming but don't. Sucks, doesn't it? Imagine if you were able to put that energy into charting a better future, one you choose for yourself that's in line with your personal mission. (That's coming in Lesson 11.)

I want you to keep track of the time and energy you spend defending yourself or counterpunching in life. I also want you to take note of how much time Jesus spends defending himself. You'll find that it's sweet little. Sure, he responds to his accusers, but when you analyze what he says, you'll discover that he uses their accusations as a teaching opportunity. He exposes all kinds of corrupt behavior. He doesn't approach his accusers from a passive position. He's assertive.

Keep track for a week. If you're a typical CNG, you'll be amazed by how much time and energy you spend in a defensive position, sometimes even explaining yourself while defending against false accusations. Remember that people do this to you because they can. And most won't stop until you do something about it. You need to become the instrument of awareness for them. (One of the most effective ways to stop it is to simply say, "Why do you say this when it's not true?" and look, don't glare, into their eyes. This way you are being both truthful and gracious, and you'll get to the heart and motive of the accusation. Whether or not the other person has enough integrity to answer honestly is another issue. Feel free to explore this if you want with additional questions, the way Jesus explored truth from falsehood.)

While keeping track of these incidents, also monitor how you feel. Chances are, you'll get all emotional though you try not to show it. Your heart rate goes up, you sweat. You may even get headaches afterward, though you attribute them to something else. You might even spend a lot of time getting angry afterward, saying to yourself all the things you want to say out loud but don't think you have the right since you don't think it's okay to defend yourself.

This exercise is a great way to discern just how much energy you spend in a damaging lifestyle. It steals your time, energy, joy, and relationships with others. You also discover that you aren't really crazy about God either, who you think keeps sending your way all these troubles when in reality you are making yourself miserable.

Now envision a life where you spend this kind of time and energy being forward moving (related to forward thinking). For example, discussing a problem with your wife or girlfriend *before* it gets out of hand. Helping your kid through a rough patch *before* it hits a crisis. Moving on to another job *before* you are forced to. These are all marks of a Christian Good Guy. Envision this successful way of living that bolsters masculinity, since you feel good about who you are for a change.

GOOD GUY WORKOUT

We must learn how to handle false accusations, stuff that's said about us that isn't true. Sometimes it's intentional, sometimes it's not. What matters most is how you handle it. For example, I just got off the phone with a book company. They mailed me the wrong book. Not the end of the world, but I needed to take care of it. I needed the book for some research I'm doing. So I called the company about the mix-up and the person on the other end told me that sometimes they let people keep the wrong book given how it sometimes costs more to return the book than what the book is worth. Then he said, "How are we supposed to know that we sent you the wrong book?"

I said, "You know because I said you did. I already have a copy of the book you sent. I don't need two of them. I really don't have the time to call you, but I'm doing it because I need the right book, not because I want to keep the wrong book."

I cut to the chase and asked them what specifically are they going to do to get me the right book ASAP. I didn't yell and I didn't demean anyone.

Now it's your turn.

The next time someone falsely accuses you, consider if it's in your best interest to challenge it or not. Again, sometimes people simply talk too much about things they don't understand. It's not your job to correct the world. But it is your job to take care of your life in a proactive manner. Sometimes saying simply, "That's not true," or "You're mistaken," is enough to change the tenor of the conversation.

GOOD GUY REBELLION ROLL CALL

Years ago, I attended a Passion Play put on by a small church. The guy who played Christ walked through the part like an emotionless robot. Later he regretted showing his bare chest during the crucifixion scene, saying that, "I save it for my wife." It's this kind of limp attitude toward Christ and masculinity that No More Christian Nice Guy *takes a stand against.*
—Carl

MASCULINITY: THE JOURNEY FROM NICE GUY TO GOOD GUY (PART 2)

L esson 10, based on chapter 10, picks up where the last lesson left off. This lesson takes a unique turn because it extols the benefits of domesticity and how, when properly handled and applied, it feeds masculinity. It also includes protecting the weak, admiring truly good people, and getting back our outrage, among other actions that fuel masculinity.

IN PRAISE OF DOMESTICITY

Read enough books on masculinity and you'll get the impression that it's found only *out there* somehow: in the boardroom, on the dock, the high seas, or with a gun or alpine rope in your hand, among other venues. No doubt, we are forged into another kind of man in these theaters, though not the best kinds of men. No matter how attached we guys get to our work or outdoor pursuits, computer, hand tool, or gun, they simply will not love us back. A woman's love grows us as men in ways we cannot receive otherwise.

But there's one place that keeps getting short-changed, partly because men feel out of place there due to a female definition of this fundamental theater.

That place is home life, the place where the fires of domesticity burn. It's how we live in the privacy of our own homes. It is a gift, and sometimes a curse, to our family, and among our most meaningful offerings to God.

For men married to women of basic goodwill:

Think about who you were before you got married, and think about the kind of man you are today. How has domesticity changed you for the better?

What kind of man do you think you would be if you didn't get married?

How has the love you've given (this includes both acts and words judged from male standards [like fixing a leaky roof], not female standards) changed the people under your care?

In what ways would you like to bless others more with your talents and abilities? Make a list and start doing them.

For single men who want to be married to a woman of basic goodwill:

What are ways that you envision home life changing you into a better man?

Talk to married men, and if they're honest, they will likely tell you that marriage forged them—often through hot fires—into better men today.

In what ways do you think you will be forged?

What weaknesses do you think will be exposed, and what can you do today to address these weaknesses?

What is required of you to ensure this transformation?

What role will being wise as a serpent play?

What role do you think fear plays in stopping this transformation?

MASCULINITY PROTECTS THE WEAK

Who are the weak people in your life? By weak, I don't mean morally weak who can't seem to stay out of trouble, either with the law or close relationships. I'm talking about people who just don't have much power in life.

How can you help them outsmart their pain and suffering?

In what ways do they need to be wise as serpents, and how can you help them obtain this insight?

What ways right now can you anticipate your children's difficulties, and what can you do to guide them through as opposed to saving them from life's necessary growth?

WEIGHT OF LIFE

Men tend to represent the weight of life to children. And sometimes, because of our aggressive tendencies (passive men have this tendency as well, but they just release it in overblown ways), we make this weight too heavy. If we aren't careful, what we intended to use to *instruct* becomes a medium through which we *destruct*.

Both our culture and our churches have told us that aggression is a bad trait. Men must strip it from their lives, we've been told, and the world suffers for this misguided message. Properly handled and focused, aggression is a positive and creative force.

Just read the first few chapters of the Gospel of John and you'll see that Jesus would not have completed his redemptive mission, fulfilling his Father's will in his life, if he had not been aggressive. Without this valuable trait, he would not have rearranged and even destroyed our many misconceptions about God. Aggression is a medium through which authority, backbone, and weight are delivered.

How can you represent this weight of life, to teach your children to focus, be aware, and change when necessary without crushing them?

We simply cannot be good fathers if we do not respect and harness our drives and instincts. Pretending they don't exist just confuses matters and sinks us further in the malaise of passivity, depression, and addiction.

How can you respect your aggressive tendencies, which for passive men often come out sideways and perverted when we pretend they don't exist, and harness them for good? (Hint: While reading about the life of Jesus, see what he does with his aggressive behavior. Does he act this way for himself, or is his purpose larger, more grand?)

Children do not start off questioning our authority. They are usually filled with a natural grace toward us fathers. But with time this can break down, often when authority gets abusive. Remember: rules without relationships lead to rebellion.

If your relationship with your children has broken down, ask yourself: Have I laid down too many rules without the relationship required for these rules to be respected?

If so, work on rebuilding your relationship with your kids, not by insisting on more rules. Show them that you care—you are in their corner.

What are specific ways that you can rekindle your relationship with your kids?

What can you do to help your kids better understand you, which will help them understand who they really are?

OUR OWN BIOGRAPHERS

We raise our own biographers, make no mistake about it. They may not write books about us that will be read by millions, but they will say things about us that will be heard by others.

What do you want your family to say about you?

What do you think they will say about you?

Do these lists line up?

If not, what can you do today to be spoken well of in the future?

PROTECTIVE, AFFIRMING WORDS

I list one example of my father's protective words on my behalf, beginning on page 174. His words filled me with a sense of protection and value. Now it's your turn.

Do you have similar words, coming from either your father or mother, that helped you realize that they were in your corner, defending you, protecting you? Try to remember how good it felt and how much bigger you were able to live.

Now, what words can you use to bolster your children today?

This section in the book also gives an example of how I witnessed a father attack his son with words that destroyed him.

If you received similar words from your father (or in my case, my mother), what did you do with them? In what ways did you pretend you weren't human, therefore they didn't affect you?

If they still burn within you, describe how they limit you.

Now let's be crime solvers, like we were earlier.

What was the lie you were told? (Note: Lies don't unravel by themselves. They take on a life of their own, mutating throughout time to claim other parts of your life and mind. They need to be confronted. Talk about them with people you trust and who know about these kinds of lies and what they do to a person's life. Expose them to truth and they will wither in its powerful light. It's part of God's grace.)

When a parent verbally demeans and attacks a kid, it's not about the kid. It's about the parent's inability to really parent, usually due to some troubles they bring into adult life.

What were the troubles that your parent(s) was affected by?

How does this shed light on the falsehood you were told?

GOOD VS. NICE

I'm asked this question a lot. What's the difference between being good and being nice? I answer this beginning on page 176.

The main issue here is how Nice Guys, often filled with good intentions, try to rescue people from their problems as opposed to helping people through their problems. This naïve approach is the standard operating system for CNGs. Among our most fatal mistakes is that we often give the suffering person too much benefit of the doubt during their struggles. Nice Guys do this a lot in relationships. They get involved with troubled women, thinking they can ride in and fix the situation, not realizing that she's the main reason problems are haunting her in the first place. He often ends up getting eaten alive, feeling resentful and jaded. But don't take my word for it. Hear it from a CNG himself.

GOOD GUY REBELLION ROLL CALL

Twenty-five years of my life have been affected by the Christian Nice Guy problem. I lost my marriage and then had to fight to get custody of my kids. I just broke up with a girl after dating for almost four years. I tried to rescue her and it cost me thousands of dollars and a lot of grief. I thought I could fix her problems, but then I realized that she was causing a lot of problems in her own life. I told her this and she left.
—Gary

Another CNG in a similar situation writes:

I've been trying to help others, but it hasn't worked out well for anyone. I think I'm pleasing God by being such a martyr. I have put myself in debt and now work two jobs to pay it off. I feel so used and I hate it!

It's hard to sleep at night and fight off depression during the day. I'm so glad I got your book. I need to focus on God's will for the rest of my life. No more of this "disease to please." I will guard my heart, learn to say "no," require respect, and mind my own business among other things. I have needs and wants just like everyone else. I'm trusting God to meet those needs and wants and help me out of the CNG mentality. Your book is a godsend. Thanks.

—Ted

In what ways have you prolonged the destructive behavior of others through your rescuing efforts that don't work?

In what ways can you let the adults in your life live their life, free of your good intentions that don't work, but with the blessing of your love and care?

BONUS INFORMATION: HEALTHY BOUNDARIES

Creating your own clear sense of self is among the best of ways to truly help others in situations like the previous letter writers. This helps you figure out where your life and responsibilities end and where others begin, which is especially helpful for CNGs who were abused or neglected as kids.

Now think in terms of the main person you have tried to rescue. In what ways have you blurred the line between who you are (your time, will, energy, and resources) and where the person you tried ro rescue begins? Fortify this distinction, and you will be on your way to becoming a Christian Good Guy.

In what ways can you rebuild the wall between who you are and who others are?

How do you think this will help them?

You also need to tell the person that you will no longer try to rescue them from their own problems. They need to face and correct their own problems. You can't do this for them. Here are some sample scripts to help you with this task:

> *In the past, I've tried to rescue you from [drinking, reckless spending, workaholism, whatever]. Along with being concerned about you, I wanted you to like me. I was sincere but unaware of what effect my efforts were having. I still want you to stop your [whatever], but I won't be trying to save you anymore.*
>
> Or:
>
> *I used to deny, cover up, and try to control your behavior. I now see how mistaken that was and I'm not going to do it anymore. I love you and want you to stop [whatever], but you'll now have to do that for yourself.* (Too Nice for Your Own Good *by Duke Robinson.*)

With this new understanding of nice vs. good, write down the name of the first Good Guy who comes to mind. If in a group, discuss why. If by yourself, tell a friend why.

MASCULINITY SEES THE WORLD CLEARLY

The word nice, you'll remember, comes from two very old and unflattering words, meaning "ignorance, an absence of knowledge or awareness." This has nothing to do with real Christianity. And it sure has nothing to do with successful living.

If we learn anything from Jesus' parable of the Shrewd Manager (Luke 16), it's that he wants us to be more aware and shrewd, not less. When you marry personal purity with shrewdness and wisdom, as Jesus commanded, your life will take off. Here's one of my favorite letters from a reader, which illustrates what I'm talking about:

> *My battle with fear intensified during my divorce. I was married for ten years, the last two being the toughest I ever had as a father to my*

sons, and as a man. My wife was fed up with our marriage and wanted me to move out. Our conversations in front of the boys turned to arguments. And the more I tried to not argue in front of the boys, she'd start them anyway, as well as physical abuse. She'd call me gay over and over, call me useless and lazy as well. I wouldn't react because . . . I didn't want to cause a scene in front of the boys. But it bothered me as I figured to them, I appeared weak.

I went to a Christian counselor and he asked me if I still wanted to try to make it work, and I said yes. It'd be a road to hoe but I made a vow to her in front of God for better or worse. However, I had a suspicion of a potential marital affair on her part, and I bugged my phone. A week later, listening to the tape, I caught her and her lawyer (I didn't know she had one) planning to have me kicked out on false child abuse charges. This way I was out, paying for everything, and I was gone from her life. I never felt so betrayed, but I didn't let on.

I found a Christian lawyer (a woman) who was fed up with the crap I was going through and told me to file a complaint on the physical abuse (read: get some backbone). But I had had enough and filed for a divorce. She would be served the day before the police were to come to "charge" me. The charade went on for four days, and the abuse continued. She'd hit me and taunt me to phone the police. I told her what goes round comes round. The day she was served, the abuse stopped. I took the wind out of her sails.

I moved out. I felt like a failure to the boys, that I couldn't keep my marriage intact. I had a fear of ever getting to see the boys and how I was going to cope. But I had an excellent counselor who kept my pity party short. I had the attitude that my sons were #1 and I'd do everything I could with God's help to help them through a terrible time. I prayed to God to give me the strength and knowledge to figure out how to make it work. God helped me to get the boys half of the time, much to my ex-wife's dismay, and everything with work fell into place. My company told me to do whatever it took to get my living arrangements and schedule to work. It's going to be four years come January, and my sons are settled in. They tell me I'm a terrific father, and I support them in all they do.

I have devotions with them and I teach them not to take crap from people who belittle them, to stand up for their beliefs and stand up for what they know is right and be a voice for what is wrong. And I've had a lot of success. My second son, with his two best friends, stood up against a group of bullies picking on the new kid in school. I got a call from his teacher. I thought he couldn't be in trouble, as my sons are known to be polite, studious, and well-liked. When I got there, she assured me he wasn't in trouble, but that he stood up to these schoolyard bullies. I said to her I'm not surprised, and I appreciated the acknowledgment for what he did. I was so proud of him, I gave him a big hug when I got home.

I learned through the whole process that someone had total control over me, tried to instill in me a fear of unfounded failure, vowed to ruin my reputation and bankrupt me, question my gender to embarrass and belittle me in front of my sons . . . and she was slowly succeeding. With my counselor, lawyer, and God's help, I got my backbone back, called her bluff, and conquered fear. I feel closer to God than ever before, and I feel I can tackle anything. I'm not proud I'm divorced, but I have a better life, and so do my sons.

—Brent, Member, Good Guy Rebellion

FACTS WE MUST NOT MISS

Note what would have happened to Brent if he hadn't been proactive, if he believed that there wasn't anything he could do against the forces mounting against him. He was an assertive hammer, not a passive anvil. He didn't *only* "pray" about the situation, then wait to see what would happen.

- He didn't go into battle alone. He surrounded himself with people who possessed greater knowledge and insight. Some men think this is a sign of weakness, which is foolish, and they (and others) pay dearly for their foolishness. This thinking is often a cheap cover for fear and other forms of emotional paralysis.

- He listened to his instincts, part of the common sense God gave him. This helped him be wise as a serpent.

- There's a misconception that there are two kinds of men: those who feel fear and those who don't. Nonsense. He felt fear—*but he didn't let what's often a deceiver and imposter stop him.* He pushed through it with proactive thinking and living.

- Note the cruelty that some women possess and that for some reason we look past. Some Christian men have been told that her bad behavior was somehow his fault.

- We consider single women as today's widows of the Bible. This needs to change to include today's single fathers as well, especially those who have had their lives destroyed by false accusations of sexual abuse against children. This is bearing false witness against another (one of the ten Commandments), which is a particular sin in America's court systems against husbands and fathers.

  Remember the wife's use of physical violence. A child is more likely to be physically abused by his mother than his father. Yet a cultural prejudice still exists against fathers in this area. We as a culture lack discernment in this area.

- Note how this deceptive woman attempted to milk the legal system against her husband, using every possible prejudice against him, colluding even with an attorney.

Now it's your turn.

Brent's story illustrates so well the importance of being proactive, shrewd, and listening to your God-given common sense and instincts.

What area of your life right now do you need to employ these qualities? Discuss them with someone who's not a CNG.

SEARCHING ONE'S SOUL AND FACING ONE'S FEARS

Fear is the Achilles tendon, glass ceiling, Ziploc bag around one's heart, and the thorn in the tiger's paw that keeps CNGs on the sidelines of life, where they stew in undisclosed resentment, anger, and rage. Though some may have an inkling as to what fear might be doing to them, many don't have a clue. Fear keeps them from conforming to the image of the true Christ, who didn't worship at the altar of other people's approval.

All they really know is that their Nice Guy script isn't working when they think that it should. When they come to this intersection of their lives, they often burn rubber in the wrong direction, blaming other people for the sorry condition of their life. How I wish they had a greater understanding of fear, the subject of today's lesson.

Facing fear is easier than it appears. I can write that now, here, on the other side of my confrontation with fear. I didn't believe it on the entry side. What paved the way for my transformation was the life-giving gift of humility. I admitted that I was out of my league, that I needed help. I needed someone or something to show me a better way to live. And what shocked me is how good this felt. I thought I'd feel horrible and ashamed. Not so, Grasshopper.

Without looking it up, write down what you think the definition of humility is. Now go look it up. (I'll help you: one definition is the quality of being modest or respectful.) If you're like most Christian Nice Guys, your definitions don't line up. As Jimi Hendrix lamented, "There must be some confusion here."

Did you think that being humble meant you had to live small and feel bad about yourself, that you had to somehow beat yourself up?

How has your faulty definition of humility, what you could call false humility, gotten you off track in life?

In what ways can being respectful toward truth, which is part of the definition of humility, broaden your horizons toward a better life?

False humility tries to get us to strangle our unique abilities and gifts. I give you an example of this from my own life, beginning on page 186. A luminary like C. S. Lewis recognized his unique abilities and saw them as a gift from God, which required greater diligence on his part. He was able to bless others better because he embraced his gifts instead of pretending through false humility that they didn't exist.

Now it's your turn.

What unique ability have you tried to downplay instead of embrace, which would help you become wise as a serpent, a better warrior of light?

How exactly did you downplay it, and what lie did you employ, helping to pervert your own discernment?

Have you asked God to forgive you for this lie and poor stewardship?

Now ask God to help you become a better steward of your gifts and talents.

GOD'S TELLING YOU SOMETHING

Earlier in the book I wrote how as an adult, I expected someone to come and hit me while showering, though no one had ever done this to me as an adult and most likely never will. I was a poster child for irrational thinking. But still it was there. If I had been truly humble, respecting the truth of this situation, I would have explored it further, and I would have created a lot less misery if I had. I simply lacked discernment, awareness, and courage.

Your mind has likely been telling you something similar. A different scenario perhaps, but a similar message: Life is not a safe place. At any moment you will be abused, neglected, ignored, or hurt somehow. This fearful scenario will appear random, as it did as a kid, and it will be void of a fundamental truth because, unlike a child, you have a say as to how you will be treated by others. Let me state this fundamental point again: You are no longer a plaything for other people. You have a say as to how people treat you, *if you will become an active participant in your own life.*

That's where the lie of abuse breaks down. That's the will of a lie. It wants you to keep believing what's not true about yourself. That you have no power, no say, no will. (See why being proactive is so important, especially in light of how fear literally freezes a person into inactivity?)

A key paradox of our Christian faith is that though we are unable to save ourselves, we must also become active agents of change and growth in our own lives. We partner with God regarding this spiritual maturity.

Now a gut question: How can you, today, become a more active participant in your own healing from the forces of fear?

 GOOD GUY WORKOUT

Search your mind for moments where you feel fear, though it really doesn't make sense.

Be humble about this fact. Respect the truth of it and don't feel ashamed about it. On one hand it's a big deal. It's a marker that will help lead you toward freedom. But on the other hand it's not a big deal. Everyone struggles with something. Everybody has some ugly in them. This revelation means you're human. There's no shame in that, remember?

Write this fear down in a simple sentence without beating yourself up in the process. Look at the truthfulness of this sentence. Don't pull back. Look at it right now and don't try to change the words.

What does this event and sentence reveal to you about fear?

To which insightful person will you turn for help, knowing that fear usually doesn't go away by itself (it often grows and mutates)?

THE BENEFITS OF OPTIMISM

As you can tell by now, I'm not crazy about sugary sweet Christianity—the kind that claims life is all rainbows and sunshine and with just a hint of rain. That just isn't real and it's not biblical—the same thing. But at the same time, we need to make sure we avoid the jaded and cynical side of life, which is a natural, though destructive, result of abuse and naïveté.

Optimism, related to hope, is linked with healthy thinking and healthy bodies. And optimism is a rare commodity in the life of a CNG.

Here are some practical ways to raise your optimism:

- Meditate on optimistic Scriptures. Chapter 11 lists some, but there's a lot more. Take out your journal and write them down as you come across them during your regular Bible studies.
- Read happier literature. Keep a regular supply of humor going through your head.
- Listen to music with an uplifting beat.

MIND YOUR BUSINESS AND LIFE MISSION

The above three ways to raise optimism are good and helpful, but they pale when compared to the next exercise, something I've mentioned earlier in this Study Guide.

Minding your own business is about growing a real life that is beneficial to you and others and brings God glory. For CNGs, this means getting past the belief that taking care of your wants and needs are somehow sinful. The following steps, designed to help you form a personal Life Mission, will ensure you don't become a selfish brute, so relax.

What in life stirs your passions (your cute wife or girlfriend doesn't count)?

Who, or what church message, has caused you to try to subvert these passions?

How can you better feed these passions?

What did you dream about before dreams felt like such a burden?

What do your friends say you're good at?

What is the pain in your heart right now?

How can you use it in the service of others, which also fills you with meaning and purpose?

What form of suffering gets under your skin the most, and how can you be wise as a serpent alleviating it?

We sometimes think that our time to grow and unveil our personal

Life Mission is in the future when we have it all together or when we gain a name with reputation. This is another way CNGs try to live perfectly, and it keeps them stuck.

What redemptive work can you do now, that calls to you now? Give this work a name. For example, I created the Good Guy Rebellion. Then give your work an action statement that summarizes your goal. For Good Guy Rebellion, this action statement is: Helping men overcome common forces that make them fearful, passive, weak, and "nice." Then list how you will go about making your Life Mission a reality. For me, it meant creating a platform (books and speaking engagements, media interviews), and sacrificing comforts like a regular income, among other changes.

What will you need to sacrifice in order to fulfill this Life Mission?

What creative struggles do you foresee?

EXPECT TO FALTER

Again, there are not two kinds of people: those who never feel fear and doubt and the rest of us who do. Expect to falter as you transform into a Christian Good Guy. One way to fortify yourself during these times of questioning and confusion is to share your Life Mission with people you trust. Ideally, share it with someone who has made a similar transformation. They will know your story intimately and should be able to offer you other valuable insights. Go to these people during the dark times, and they will help keep you on the right path. And regular, even un-dramatic, steps toward fulfilling your Life Mission is a proven way to fight off depression and feed hope and optimism.

EMBRACING CHANGE

All these lessons will largely be a waste of your time if you choose spiritual stagnation and sin over spiritual growth and maturity. Most people just seem to hate change, more so for CNGs who are attached to their comfort zones, even though they reduce and demean them and stop them from conforming to the image of Christ.

Jesus asked the man at the pool of Bethesda, "Do you want to get well?" This passage used to puzzle me, until I saw what people actually do as opposed to what they say they want.

Do you really want to get well?

How can you tell if someone is serious about change in their life?

What specifically do you fear about change?

Is this fear justified, or is it like most fears false?

Because courage, will, and inspiration are required to embrace change in your life, who are the people in your life who show these qualities, and what can you learn from them? (Hint: If you don't know any, visit the biography section of your library or bookstore.)

NO MORE MR. NICE GUY: PRACTICAL HELP FOR YOUR NEW LIFE AHEAD

This lesson, based on chapter 12, provides practical information you need to live the Christian Good Guy lifestyle, a way of living that doesn't beg or bully. It's the assertive way to live, the way our Savior did, who we do well to think of as the Assertive One.

GOOD GUY WORKOUT

Think of your life as a garden. It helps if you have gardening experience. If not, let me tell you a few things as an amateur gardener. Those beautiful and plush photos you see of gardens in magazines and books? They take work! Expert gardeners give great care to their plants and it shows. They discern what's happening and they anticipate trouble. Expert gardeners are a proactive group.

Weeds are nothing more than living things that don't suit the purpose of the gardener. They aren't bad. They just don't fit. They are the wrong plant in the wrong place. They clash with the overall mission of the gardener, and they do not cry when we pull them up.

Success in most cases most of the time is not accidental. Sure, some people have wealth handed to them on a silver platter. But the majority of people who do well (and I'm not just talking wealth) are diligent people. They share many of the qualities of fruitful gardeners.

Envision your life as a raised garden bed. Do a quick drawing if you want. And in this bed are plants you want to grow healthy and strong (your understanding of God, wife, children, career, your healthy desires, and so on). Yet there are other plants growing in your garden-life as well. They are weeds, which pull life-giving sustenance from the plants you want to grow. Some can actually kill your plants, but more often than not they impair and obstruct. They hinder your plants from an abundant existence.

Give these weeds, which will be a combination of internal and external forces, a name.

How long have they been in your garden? This is good to know because the older ones will be harder to pull.

What will be the most effective way to get rid of them?

How can you limit their growth in the future?

What can you do to fertilize the plants you want to grow?

DECLARATION OF INDEPENDENCE

Ruth Koch and Kenneth Haugk wrote an insightful message to Christians who think it's a sin to be human, found on page 201. Read it out loud. Study it and make sure to reference the Scriptures that are included. This will help you realize that you have intrinsic rights and value, being made in the image of God.

This personal Declaration of Independence will help you become more comfortable, making your requests of others clear and confident. One of the best ways to do this is to tell people what you want, but in a concise manner.

So think about something you want right now that fits your Life Mission. Write it down. Now let's do some editing. Start the sentence with "I want," then state the object of your want. If the object of your desire involves another person who you think is standing in your way, make sure that you don't shame or blame this person. That just shuts their ears down to your legitimate request, and it really isn't the purpose of your request (at least it shouldn't be: remember, we're not seeking revenge, we're seeking a resolution that's good for everyone if possible).

Now we get to the why statement, which is often required for good communication. In the same sentence, state why you want what you want and make sure it is not apologetic. Then the clincher: make a demand upon the person that, again, doesn't shame or blame but instead charts a path toward true resolution of the problem. This will help you become a *true* peacemaker, since real peace is often forged through conflict, not by simply rolling over.

So, for example, let's say you want to stop someone from being disrespectful toward you. Your two-sentence request may look like this:

I want you to stop yelling at me because it's disrespectful and demeaning. What are you going to do to ensure that this problem won't happen again?

Why is being demeaned and disrespected not part of your Life Mission? Because it wastes valuable energy and time and leads to the sins of resentment and bitterness. And it allows the destructive sin of another person to go unchallenged. This pulls you from the better life you are responsible to chart. And abusive people need help, just like you. Many don't know how to have a real relationship. They need people like you, experts on disrespect, to help them learn how to become respectful.

Expect to make this statement more than once, since many abusive people don't want you to accept your definition of your relationship. They want you to accept *their* definition. And if they blow up at you, tell them that you look forward to getting their answer later and end the conversation. If you have to hang up or walk away, do so. You are not required to take additional abuse.

TEN CGG PRINCIPLES TO LIVE BY

The start of a new year is the traditional time people vow to make changes in their lives. The problem is, those resolutions often don't stick. No matter when you're going through this Study Guide, let me challenge you to follow these principles and stand resolute in your desire to be a Christian Good Guy.

1. I will confront the causes of fear that keep me shackled, alone, resentful, and unable to love and be loved. Fear, I'll remind myself, wants to render me nice and innocuous.
2. I will speak the truth in love and without apology—especially to people who abuse me.
3. I will remember what one person living bravely looks like in a crowd. It's a lot of fun.
4. I will no longer worship at the altar of other people's approval. Instead, I will sacrifice, not so others will like me, but because it's good for them and me and brings God pleasure.
5. In order to become a redemptive force for good, I will become wise, shrewd, and cunning like a serpent, knowing that personal piety alone doesn't cut it in life.
6. I will underline in my Bible where God and others aren't nice but good. This will give me strength and inspiration and help me become the right kind of dangerous.
7. I will not run from my emotions, knowing they are valuable messengers. They make me more alive and more like Jesus, who was more emotional and passionate than those around him.
8. I will remember that anger often stems from fear. When angry I will ask myself: What do I fear? Is this fear real or part of a deception?
9. I will remember that passivity is often the sin of omission in

disguise. Though others may be fooled by this deception, God isn't.

10. Because I'm made in the image of God, I will no longer think that I'm worthless, and I will take care of myself, knowing it's not a sin.

LIVING WELL TAKES COURAGE

Contrary to conventional wisdom, living well takes courage, because it's harder to do what needs to be done to live well than to keep feeling bad. Feeling good, having energy, being excited about life, and donating a part of yourself to others freely happens when you actively participate in the quality of your life and when you see the quality increase due to these efforts. For CNGs, this means moving into areas of life that make you uncomfortable but that you know will improve the quality of your days. The more you do it, the easier it becomes.

Statistically, there are more unhappy people than happy ones. Being unhappy requires much less of you than does being happy; feeling good involves the courage not to fold in the face of life's disappointments, frustrations, opposition, or just plain misunderstandings.

Being loving and good, which is at the core of the Good Guy Rebellion, is not for the weak at heart. It requires strength that niceness saps from you.

In what physical, emotional, and spiritual ways does your niceness sap you of power and courage?

OH BABY, CHRISTIAN TESTIMONIES

Straight-talking pastor Steve Brown sets a lot of CNGs free when he warns against the unintentional tyranny of false Christian testimonies, which creates false comparisons and robs you of your boldness. This is found on page 204.

Think about the testimonies you've heard at church that seemed too good to be true. (This doesn't mean you don't believe in miracles or God's divine intervention. It does mean that you question the person's testimony about such things.)

Did you make yourself believe in this questionable testimony, even though your God-given common sense told you otherwise? If so, why did you lie to yourself?

How have false testimonies been a form of tyranny in your life?

If in the future you hear what you think is a questionable testimony, go up to the person afterward and ask him some questions. One thing's for sure: one of you will walk away enlightened.

ENRAGED BY STRENGTH

I wish I could tell you that your transformation from a CNG to a Christian Good Guy will be accompanied by nothing but wild applause and dancing in the streets. You know by now that this isn't true. Jesus said that this world will come with its share of problems, especially when you try to do the right thing.

Part of being wise as a serpent means anticipating problems and doing what you can to offset them.

So think about the people in your life who like you soft and nice.

What do you think they will say and do about the new you?

How did Jesus handle people who came against him because he was a redemptive force for good?

What, if anything, can you do to wisely, not fearfully, protect yourself from what you sense is coming?

What can you do today to not look back on the past with anger, but instead look forward without fear and look around in awareness?

NATION OF WIMPS

We are raising another generation of Christian weaklings: kids who are told that having a backbone, will, opinions, and unique gifts and skills are somehow arrogant and "worldly." I call them spiritual veal. Their parents go through great lengths to keep them from the inevitable bumps and bruises of life. In their earnest desire to keep children from life's hard side, they make them timid and fearful people.

In what ways do kids need to feel badly sometimes?

In what ways are Christians particularly overprotective of their kids?

Instead of trying to keep your kid from hardships, how can you help him *through* the hardship, so he'll be a stronger person?

Is your child more or less: responsive to the herd, willing to disagree with his peers, eager to fit in, assertive, questioning of authority?

How did Jesus handle these aspects of life?

How can you live out more examples of the tough side of your faith so as to model the right kind of living?

FOCUSING ON THE F-WORD

Life isn't "fair." One aspect that makes life so difficult is that sometimes it can be immensely *unfair*. This gets under the skin of CNGs because they think that if they can discover the secret formula of life, someday it will be trouble free. You know by now that this is wishful thinking.

What ways can you chart a brighter future despite unfairness?

What did Jesus do in the face of unfairness?

How does being wise as a serpent play a role in this important work?

CHOOSING PASSIVITY

Choosing to withdraw your will from a given situation can be a proactive and assertive action. Page 214 lists some situations in which choosing to not assert yourself might be best.

Read through this list and ask yourself: Which situation on this list is likely to present itself in my life soon?

This will help you respond with necessary grace when and if the situation comes around.

FINAL THOUGHT

If you are part of a group going through this Study Guide, you will now have shared your deepest pain, and you'll possess a greater level of hope, love, and faith. If you have completed this Study Guide on your own, you too have been encouraged to share your thoughts with an inner group of people, your own personal tribe, to help you become a Christian Good Guy. To both groups, congratulations!

Keep your friendships going because, as I write at the end of chapter 12, you will need the support of others to keep you on the Christian Good Guy journey. This journey is a series of plateaus, not finish lines. And with the support of others—people with whom you share your victories and temporary setbacks—you will continue to be the right kind of dangerous. Just like Jesus.

JESUS THE NAUGHTY NAZARENE

The master commended the dishonest manager because he had acted shrewdly. For the people of this world are more shrewd in dealing with their own kind than are the people of the light.
—Jesus, in the parable of the Shrewd Manager (Luke 16:8)

Eugene Peterson's *The Message* translates this unique parable this way: "Now here's a surprise: The master praised the crooked manager! And why? Because he knew how to look after himself. Streetwise people are smarter in this regard than law-abiding citizens. They are on constant alert, looking for angles, surviving by their wits. I want you to be smart in the same way—but for what is *right*—using every adversity to stimulate you to creative survival, to concentrate your attention on the bare essentials, so you'll live, really live, *and not complacently just get by on good behavior*" (emphasis added).

There is no greater portion of Scripture that shows CNGs that it's no sin being wise and shrewd. As *No More Christian Nice Guy* states over and over: *Good behavior alone doesn't cut it in life, men!* It needs to be married with intelligent and creative proactive living.

Chances are, you never heard a sermon based on this parable. It isn't "nice," but it sure is good for the lives of CNGs—and those who love and rely upon them.

Can't you just hear the good church folk gasp if Jesus preached this parable from the pulpit this Sunday?

CNGs, you need to balance this score, and don't expect the church to lead in this area. You and fellow members of the Good Guy Rebellion will have to do it.

GOOD GUY REBELLION ROLL CALL

> *The Christian Nice Guy problem matters to me because it nega-tively affects too many areas of my life, particularly relationships with women and work. I shared some of the ideas in* No More Chris-tian Nice Guy *with a friend of mine and he went out and bought the book too. We enjoy discussing your book with each other and try to help one another to grow out of our CNG way of thinking, doing, and relating. Thanks for writing it!*
> —Michael

RECOMMENDED RESOURCES
FOR FURTHER ADVANCEMENT

BOOKS

Dr. Laura Schlessinger, *The Proper Care and Feeding of Husbands* (New York: Harper Collins, 2004).

John Eldredge, *Wild at Heart* (Nashville: Thomas Nelson, 2001).

Dr. Robert Glover, *No More Mr. Nice Guy: A Proven Plan for Getting What You Want in Love, Sex, and Life* (Philadelphia: Running Press, 2003).

Mark O'Connell, Ph.D., *The Good Father* (New York: Scribner, 2005).

Ruth N. Koch and Kenneth C. Haugk, *Speaking the Truth in Love: How to Be an Assertive Christian* (St. Louis, Mo: Stephen Ministries, 1992).

Marvin Allen with Jo Robinson, *Angry Men, Passive Men: Understanding the Roots of Men's Anger and How to Move Beyond It* (New York: Fawcett Columbine, 1993).

Bruce Barton, *The Man Nobody Knows* (Indianapolis: Bobbs-Merrill Company, 1925).

Robert Inchausti, *Subversive Orthodoxy: Outlaws, Revolutionaries and Other Christians in Disguise* (Grand Rapids, Mich: Brazos Press 2005).

Rabbi Shmuely Boteach, *Face Your Fear: Living with Courage in an Age of Caution* (New York: St. Martin's Press, 2004).

Elton Trueblood, *The Humor of Christ: A Bold Challenge to the Traditional Sterotype of a Somber, Gloomy Christ* (New York: Harper & Row, 1964).

Dr. James Dobson, *Love Must Be Tough* (Waco, Tex: Word Books, 1983).

Anne Lamott, *Traveling Mercies* (New York: Pantheon Books, 1999).

Stephen Oates, *Let The Trumpet Sound: Life of Martin Luther King Jr.* (New York: Harper & Row, 1982).

Dr. Lawrence Crabb, *The Silence of Adam* (Grand Rapids, Mich: Zondervan, 1995).

Dr. Dan B. Allender and Dr. Tremper Longman III, *Bold Love* (Colorado Springs: Nav Press, 1992).

Nicky Cruz, *Soul Obsession* (Colorado Springs: Waterbrook Press, 2005).

G. K. Chesterton, *Orthodoxy* (London: John Lane, 1909).

David Murrow, *Why Men Hate Going to Church* (Nashville: Nelson Books, 2005).

Robert and Pamela Crosby, *Now We're Talking* (Colorado Springs: Focus on the Family, 1996).

Gary Thomas, *Sacred Marriage* (Grand Rapids, Mich: Zondervan, 2000).

Mark Galli, *Jesus Mean and Wild* (Grand Rapids, Mich: Baker Books, 2006).

MUSIC

"Crash" by Dave Matthews. If married, listen and think about your wife. Many songs by Bob Seger and the Silver Bullet Band. I don't think anyone sings about a man's innate desires, hopes, and frustrations in a popular context like he does.

MOVIES, TELEVISION, AND RELATED MEDIA

Like with all media, this is not an endorsement of entire content, but rather themes and issues explored on film. For example, I'm not a big fan of violent movies. This change took place soon after having children. But sometimes violent movies contain truth we need to heed to be wise as serpents in order to truly help ourselves, others, and avoid unnecessary violence.

Little House on the Prairie (Don't let it fool you, Pa's a *man.*)
Fight Club (See what happens when masculinity is misspent.)
Weather Man (Behold the poison of passivity and naïveté.)
The Cosby Show
What About Bob? (Needy people do some wacky things.)
Saving Private Ryan
Open Range
In Good Company
We Were Soldiers Once
Backyard Drills DVD: Coaching Your Kids to Succeed on the Field of Play and in the Game of Life (www.backyarddrills.com).